JESUS WALK

DISCIPLE'S MANUAL

EDITED BY MICHAEL L. BAKER

Library of Congress Catalog Card Number: 98-068790

ISBN: 0-87148-4552

Cleveland, Tennessee 37311

Printed in the United States of America

CONTENTS

FOREWORD

The church is made up of people—individuals who have responded to the call of Christ to follow Him. In Matthew 28:18-20, Christ's command to His church was to produce a fruit-bearing believer called a *disciple.*

Recognizing that God calls believers into a variety of vocations and ministries, the church must accept its responsibility to nurture believers to identify and develop their unique spiritual gifts God has given for the expansion of His kingdom. The church must lead believers to live an abundant life in the Spirit.

Discipleship is personal spiritual growth and maturity that leads to a deepening relationship with God. It includes learning the Bible's teachings and living out those teachings in daily life. *JESUS WALK* will help lead new believers to grow in their walk with Christ. This study will assist in drawing new converts toward involvement in the varied ministries of the church fulfilling the Great Commission.

The imperative command of Christ is to "go and make disciples of all nations" (Matthew 28:19). It is a call—a call to serve. The primary calling is to share the "good news" leading others to follow Him. It is the formula for evangelizing the world. Trained and committed disciples are the work force of God and discipleship is the heart of the church.

When you have completed *JESUS WALK* your life will be changed because you will have learned to walk daily with Jesus in a new dimension of love and understanding. You will have a greater appreciation for your personal spiritual gifts and the potential you have to impact the world in the 21st century.

Paul L. Walker, Ph.D.

INTRODUCTION

PURPOSE

JESUS WALK is a twelve lesson interactive study for new believers. It is designed for use with small groups or personal individual study. The purpose of the course is to help new converts acknowledge Jesus Christ as Savior and Lord of their life. It will serve as a guide and encourager for the new disciple and will share the biblical principles important for a deeper walk with God.

SMALL GROUPS

The study groups can vary in size. The suggested group size is no more than fifteen. In addition, the study can be completed individually. However, small study groups allow for greater interaction between students and instructor.

Within the life of a church, many new believers are being brought into the kingdom on a regular basis. An important key to spiritual growth and development is the implementation of a perpetual discipleship program and ministry. *JESUS WALK* is designed for twelve sessions with the possibility of multiple discipleship-training groups operating simultaneously based upon need. There may be an immediate need to begin a new discipleship-training group and within a few weeks there are more new converts who need to begin their discipleship study. At any one point in time, there could be many different small groups meeting simultaneously in discipleship ministry.

STUDY FORMAT

JESUS WALK is an interactive study written in simple and understandable language. It includes essential elements and sections common to each lesson. Included in the lesson format are the following elements:

INTRODUCTION. An *introduction* to the discipleship topic is presented along with other topic headings throughout the study lesson.

SCRIPTURAL FOCUS. The *scriptural focus* provides scriptural references directly related to the topic discussion. All scripture quotations are NKJV (New King James Version) throughout unless otherwise noted.

APPLYING THE TRUTH—My Daily Walk with Christ. These sections call for specific action steps or interactive response to the topic discussion. Many of the activities are designed to lead the student to interaction with God through meditation, prayer, commitment and Bible study.

LESSON REVIEW. The *lesson review* succinctly summaries the topic of the lesson and brings to a conclusion the discussion.

DISCIPLESHIP INSIGHTS. These concise statements share the heart of the lesson. When each lesson is completed, these insights help the student to remember and understand key issues that were presented and discussed.

NOTES and *RESOURCES*. Each lesson provides space for personal notes, as well as, reference of resource materials for further study.

WHERE AND WHEN

The discipleship program can utilize multiple delivery systems to accommodate the differences in learning style and lifestyles of new believers. For example, sessions could be scheduled during regular church services, Sunday school, weekday mornings or evenings, before or after work or in a designated home. Where and when sessions are scheduled can be determined by the group to meet their specific needs. It should be noted that flexibility in scheduling will help to determine a "right" time and place. Regardless of what is chosen, there may be adjustments.

PARTICIPATION

Study materials in *JESUS WALK* are self-paced and interactive. Students are encouraged to study and pray prior to each scheduled meeting of the group. Attendance is important for both the student and group. Each discipleship student should make a firm commitment of participation.

RESOURCES NEEDED

Each member of the group will need a copy of the Disciple's Manual and their Bible. Students may desire to use other personal materials for notes and further study. The instructor's guide is provided as a separate volume.

Michael L. Baker, Editor

DISCIPLESHIP

A Call to Serve

LESSON 1

Michael L. Baker

INTRODUCTION

God's purpose is that we have meaning in life as we direct our daily walk and hearts toward Him. However, our sinful nature keeps us from fulfilling God's purpose for our existence. While we are all sinners by nature and by choice (Romans 3:23), God has made provision for the forgiveness of our sin.

God's Provision *Jesus Christ*

The "good news" message is that God offers that provision in His Son, Jesus Christ, who became like us to show us, how, we might become like Him. Jesus was God-man, He was God, yet He became human (John 1:1, 14). Jesus shed His blood on the cross (1 Peter 3:18) once and for all to bring us to God and was raised to life again for our justification (Romans 4:25).

Salvation

The only way we can have meaning in life is to accept Jesus Christ as Lord. John 1:12 says, "But as many as received Him, to them He gave the right to become children of God, to those who believe in His name." When we repent of our sins (salvation) and place our faith in Jesus Christ, we must completely surrender to Him as Lord. Surrender is giving Christ control of our lives. It is identifying with Him and following Him in our daily walk. We then become a part of the family of God.

Discipleship

But you may ask, "Now that I have been saved and I am a part of the family of God, what comes next? What is this thing called discipleship? What's a disciple? What is it that I need to do to become a committed follower of Jesus?" This lesson will examine the Biblical dimensions of discipleship and really what's it all about. It will take a look at a disciple's profile and characteristics that Jesus asked for in followers. In addition, it will explore the stages of discipleship development and the practical focus of discipleship as followers who understand commitment, comprehend the value of spiritual maturation and the empowerment of Spirit-filled believers for daily service.

DIMENSIONS OF DISCIPLESHIP

WHAT IS A DISCIPLE?

The Meaning of Disciple

The word *disciple* as used in the New Testament comes from the Greek word *mathetes*, which means "learner," "pupil" or "student." In the Greek language it referred to a "student" who would join or attach himself to a teacher. In the Jewish tradition contemporary to the time of Christ, a student would join himself to a teacher to learn the Scriptures. The goal of the student was to become a teacher in his own right and usually continue the traditions of his teacher or master.

Follower of Christ

In the New Testament, the word *disciple* takes on new significance because of its relationship with Jesus. The term *disciple* is used primarily to identify followers of Jesus Christ. It is also used to describe the "Twelve Disciples" or "apostles," however; the most common usage refers to those who were followers, learners, pupils, students or believers of Christ. The common usage in today's language refers to a disciple of Jesus as a committed Christian believer.

Christ the Teacher

Both *disciple* and *teacher* go hand in hand. The disciple is the learner of the teacher's doctrine. Jesus was viewed by those around Him as a rabbi or teacher (John 1:38; Mark 9:5). It is in this context that the followers or disciples of Jesus beheld Him as Master who spoke with authority. The centerpiece of New Testament discipleship is Jesus Christ, the teacher, with whom disciples or followers are called to serve. Following Christ as a disciple meant that one was committed to live according to the teachings of Jesus and share the "good news" message with others. It is a call to "discipleship" and total surrender of one's self to the teachings and example of the master—Jesus Christ (Luke 14:25-35).

A CALL TO SERVE

Jesus was walking by the Sea of Galilee and saw two brothers, Simon Peter and Andrew, casting a net into the waters. They were at their daily tasks as fishermen. Jesus spoke to them and said, "Follow Me, and I will make you fishers of men." The scriptures further state, "They immediately left their nets and followed Him" (Matthew 4:18-20).

Acceptance of the Call

The disciples of Christ literally began to walk with Him as they journeyed. He taught as they followed. It was a daily walk with Christ. It was a *Jesus Walk*. However, "following" was much more than just bodily moving along with Jesus from place to place. Acceptance of the call to follow meant listening to Him, a willingness to learn, growing in understanding and obeying His teachings.

THE DISCIPLE'S PROFILE

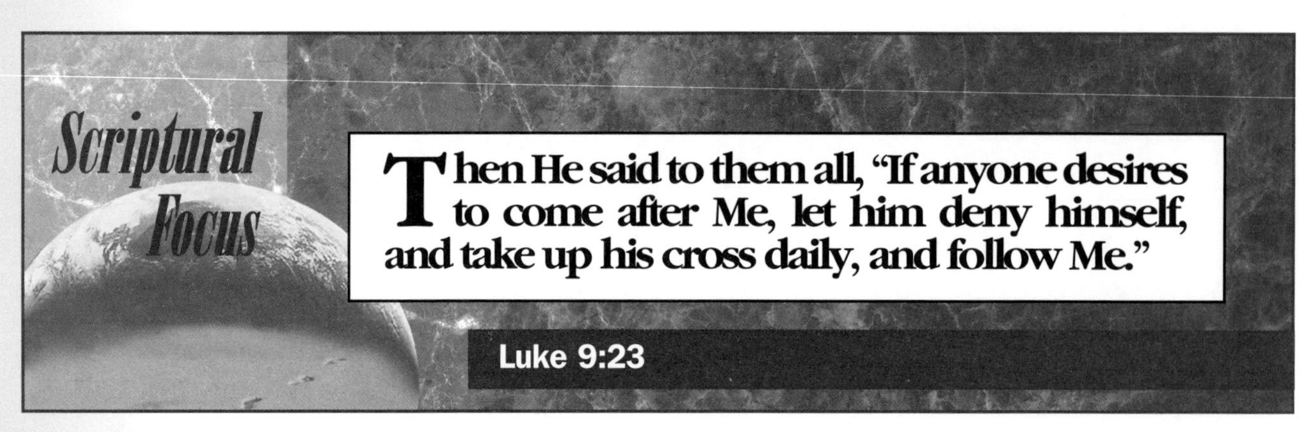

A *profile* is defined as a view of anything in contour; it is a character sketch; or presenting or summarizing data relevant to a particular person. Jesus clearly describes the profile of a disciple in Luke 9:23. It is one thing to be just a believer or convert. It is something entirely different to be a disciple. Disciples must do more than just believe. There are many that believe but never commit themselves to adjust their lifestyle and follow Christ.

Jesus characterized disciples in Luke 9:23. With the words *all* and *anyone*, Jesus does not exclude a single person. He is encouraging every believer to become a committed follower. Again, with words such as *wishes* and *let him*, Jesus is calling for an unquestionable decision to follow Him and walk in His steps. Discipleship is not just for new converts. It is a call for all to serve—both ministers and laity (Mark 8:34).

Essentials of Discipleship

He then lists three essentials of discipleship. A disciple must "deny himself," "take up his cross daily," and "follow Me." William Barclay states in *The Gospel of Matthew*, "To deny oneself means in every moment of life to say no to self, and to say yes to God. To deny oneself means once, finally and for all to dethrone self and to enthrone God" (p. 167). A disciple must follow Christ faithfully and give up self-interest in daily obedience.

✦ Deny Self

✦ Take Up Your Cross

When anyone hears the concept of "taking up a cross," the brake lights come on and caution becomes the norm. Adding to caution then comes the directions to do this "daily." Disciples from Galilee knew what the cross meant, for hundreds of men had been crucified by this means in their region. Jesus was asking believers to daily crucify their own selfishness and personal desires, take up their personal cross of commitment and give complete dedication and willing obedience to Him (Matthew 10:38).

✦ Follow Me

Jesus then concludes this profile by saying, "and follow Me." Disciples are individuals who attach themselves to Christ and desire to develop the characteristics of Christlike living. They embark on their daily walk with Jesus in perseverance. When adversity comes—they continue steadfast in their faith.

When things are good and when they are bad, a disciple keeps moving forward—they keep following—even to the end.

DISCIPLE'S PROFILE

A Disciple Is . . .

A disciple is one who . . .

- Identifies with Christ;
- Abandons self-interest;
- Bears fruit;
- Glorifies God;
- Follows Jesus in love, faith, and obedience;
- Studies the Word of God and carries it out in daily living;
- Loves as Christ loves;
- Understands the importance of and practices prayer;
- Lives a life of selfless service to God and others;
- Shares the "good news" with the world; and
- Is totally surrendered to Christ.

Applying the Truth

MY DAILY WALK WITH GOD

Ask yourself the following questions and respond *yes* or *no*.

☐ *Yes* ☐ *No* Do I really want to be a disciple?

☐ *Yes* ☐ *No* Am I willing to deny myself, take up my cross and follow Jesus?

☐ *Yes* ☐ *No* Is there something keeping me from becoming a disciple?

☐ *Yes* ☐ *No* Am I ready to accept Christ's call to serve?

Pray and accept the call to follow Jesus as a committed disciple and walk with Him daily.

BECOMING A DISCIPLE

Call to Serve

How does one become a committed disciple? The first step is to accept the call of Christ as Lord and Savior of their life. Second, accept the call to serve.

In other words, an individual finds Christ, begins a loving relationship with Him and begins to discover their gifts of serving in the Kingdom of God.

Discipleship Is a Process

Discipleship is not a program it is a process. It's a process of growing and maturing in one's relationship with Jesus. The process begins at "new birth" or "spiritual birth." This is often referred to as "being born again." New Christian believers are ordinary people; however, they have extraordinary potential as servants of Christ.

The process of discipleship is gradual and is a lifetime endeavor. Just as physical growth develops from infancy to adulthood, the spiritual life as a disciple develops from first steps as a new believer to a mature partner in ministry. No two people are exactly alike and similarly no two disciples are identical. Rather, disciples develop at different rates and times. Some move forward in the maturation process very quickly while others progress at varied paces. Regardless of the development rate, each believer has unique and special talents and abilities to use in ministry as a follower of Christ.

STAGES OF DISCIPLESHIP DEVELOPMENT

Unbelievers

There are several stages of discipleship development in the process of becoming a disciple. First, there are those who are unbelievers. They have never made a commitment to Jesus as Savior and Lord of their life. It is the responsibility of disciples to reach out to unbelievers in friendship and witness. Prayer, love and care are hallmarks for the disciple to remember as they minister to unbelievers.

Believers

Second, a new believer has made a commitment to Jesus Christ as Savior but has just begun their daily walk with Him. Every new believer begins as a spiritual infant and needs to be nurtured with the "milk" of God's Word (1 Corinthians 3:1, 2). Just as a mother and baby develop a relationship, similarly, Christ and the new believer establish a love and faith relationship. New believers are just beginning their journey.

Disciples

Third, disciples are individuals who attach themselves to Christ; mature in the spiritual disciplines (prayer, worship, stewardship, relationships, etc.); discover the gifts Christ has bestowed upon them; and finds a place of service in ministry. Developing disciples are just that—developing. In their walk with Jesus they evidence spiritual maturity, bear fruit and demonstrate a life of service under the empowerment of the Holy Spirit. As disciples grow, they hunger to learn and develop in their Christian growth. They are daily being transformed in their continuing relationship and walk with Jesus and others.

Disciplers

Fourth, disciples become disciplers. As disciples mature they find ways and means to manifest their spiritual gifts as servant leaders. The servant leader disciple is committed to teach and train other disciples in their Christian growth. As this stage progresses, the discipler and those being discipled develop mutual dependence on and service to one another as they become partners—laborers together—in ministry.

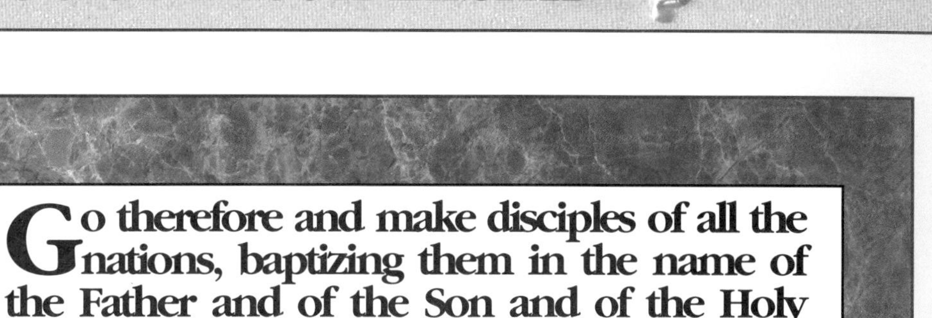

Scriptural Focus

Go therefore and make disciples of all the nations, baptizing them in the name of the Father and of the Son and of the Holy Spirit, teaching them to observe all things that I have commanded you; and lo, I am with you always, even to the end of the age. Amen.

Matthew 28:19, 20

Great Commission

At the end of Christ's earthly ministry and just before His ascension, He delivered the Great Commission to His disciples. The scriptural mandate of the Great Commission is Christ's command to the church—to disciples. In Mark 16:15, Jesus commissioned the Eleven disciples with these words, "And He said to them, 'Go into all the world and preach the gospel to every creature.'" Jesus' last message to His disciples was a call to evangelize. It was the call to "go into all the world and preach the gospel." This is also the call to every 21st century disciple. It is a call to disciple making. Bill Hull in *The Disciple Making Pastor* states, "Disciple making is the heart of the church, because it is the heart of the Great Commission" (p. 53).

COMMITMENT

A Personal Decision

A disciple who wishes to develop into a mature discipler must understand the meaning of commitment. Commitment can simply be defined as a pledge or promise to do something. It is a "self" issue. No one can give you a measure of commitment or even make you to be committed. It is a personal and conscious decision. Spiritual growth and development begins with honest commitment.

Surrender to Christ

A committed disciple demonstrates their surrender to Jesus Christ by entrusting their gifts and talents to ministry. This is accomplished through active involvement in the church—Christ's body. They recognize the importance of church attendance, worship, stewardship, Bible study, interpersonal relationships and assimilation into the church through membership. Commitment as a disciple understands the value of evangelism and fulfilling the command of Christ to "Go therefore and make disciples of all the nations" (Matthew 28:18). Jesus prayed to the Father for His disciples with these words, "As You sent Me into the world, I also have sent them into the world" (John 17:18). Jesus repeatedly issued a call, a command or a directive to "go," to "make" or to "send." However, it is our choice—our decision—our commitment to "go" and share the gospel or to "make disciples."

Evidences of Commitment

The decision to be committed is only the first step. The daily walk with Jesus and following Him is an ongoing process. The evidence of such commitment can be seen in respect for the Bible—the divinely inspired, infallible Word of God revealed to man. It is demonstrated in a willingness of disciples to duplicate themselves by becoming disciple makers. Further, it is profoundly visible by obediently denying self, bearing fruit and reproducing believers.

MATURITY

Ephesians 4:11-16 explains the disciple's journey to spiritual maturity.

> And He Himself gave some to be apostles, some prophets, some evangelists and some pastors and teachers, for the equipping of the saints for the work of ministry, for the edifying of the body of Christ, till we all come to the unity of the faith and of the knowledge of the Son of God, to a perfect man, to the measure of the stature of the fullness of Christ; that we should no longer be children, tossed to and from and carried about with every wind of doctrine, by the trickery of men, in the cunning craftiness of deceitful plotting, but, speaking the truth in love, may grow up in all things into Him who is the head—Christ—from whom the whole body, joined and knit together by what every joint supplies, according to the effective working by which every part does its share, causes growth of the body for the edifying of itself in love (Ephesians 4:11-16).

Requires a Decision

Maturity has at the core if its meaning the concept of being fully or highly developed. Jesus taught the importance of the quality of the disciple's development and spiritual maturation. Christian growth and maturity are described by phrases such as "a deeper walk with the Lord," or "a richer fellowship with Christ," or "a stronger sense of direction and calling." Yet, spiritual maturation does not just happen. It requires a decision and commitment to personal Christian growth. Churches are filled with believers who regularly attend services but have never made a commitment to discipleship and spiritual maturity.

Equipping Believers

Christ gives gifts to His church for a purpose—to equip believers to accomplish the work of ministry and thus realize the goal of building up the church. Every believer—every disciple—is called to do the work of ministry and build up the body of Christ. Paul said in verse 16, "From whom the whole body, joined and knit together by what every joint supplies, according to the effective working by which every part does its share, causes the growth of the body." Every single disciple committed, working effectively and doing their share demonstrates spiritual maturity with the outcome of Christian growth. Christ's goal is that the equipping of believers, ministering one to another in love and building up the church will continue until complete maturity is achieved.

EMPOWERMENT

The Holy Spirit working in an individual's life and the disciple's response to the Spirit are major factors. The book of Acts in the New Testament speaks much about the Spirit-filled life. Acts 13:52 says, "And the disciples were filled with joy and with the Holy Spirit." Ephesians 5:18 commands, ". . . be filled with Holy Spirit." In Luke 24:49, Jesus told His disciples to "tarry in the city of Jerusalem until you are endued with power from on high."

Spirit-filled Life

In Acts 1:8, Jesus declares, "But you shall receive power when the Holy Spirit has come upon you; and you shall be witnesses to Me in Jerusalem, and in all Judea and Samaria, and to the end of the earth." Jesus called the disciples to their first priority, which was to be witnesses of Him to the ends of the earth. He promised the Holy Spirit would come upon them and empower them for the tasks that lay ahead.

First Priority *Witness*

The nature of this power, *dunamin*, supplies the root of English words such as dynamic, dynamo and dynamite. This power is a personal enduement that comes from the indwelling of the Holy Spirit into our lives. A disciple who is baptized or filled with the Holy Spirit is empowered to testify (witness) of Jesus Christ. Christ's disciples are empowered by the indwelling of the Spirit and it brings supernatural dynamic capacity for witness and service.

dunamin

Applying the Truth

MY DAILY WALK WITH GOD

- Take time to examine your life and look for anything that may be keeping you from focusing on Christ's call to be a committed disciple.
- Ask yourself, "Where am I in my development as a disciple?" Answer the question honestly. Then lay your answer before Christ and pray for empowerment to serve.
- List any barriers that may be in your way to deter your Christian growth and development as a committed, maturing and empowered disciple.

____

____

____

____

____

____

LESSON REVIEW

God has made a provision through His Son, Jesus Christ for the forgiveness of our sin. When we repent of our sins and place faith in Jesus, we must completely surrender to Him as Lord and become a committed follower or disciple. The centerpiece of discipleship is Jesus Christ, the teacher, with whom disciples or followers are called to serve. It is a call to "discipleship" and total surrender of one's self to the teachings and example of the master—Jesus Christ.

There are three essentials of discipleship. First, a disciple must follow Christ faithfully and give up self-interest in daily obedience. Second, Jesus asks believers to daily crucify their own selfishness and personal desires, take up their personal cross of commitment and give complete dedication and willing obedience to Him. Third, disciples must follow Jesus and embark on their daily walk with Him.

Discipleship is not a program it is a process. It is a gradual lifetime endeavor. Stages of discipleship development include unbelievers, new believers, disciples and disciplers.

The focus of discipleship begins with the mandate of the Great Commission (Matthew 28:18-20). The committed disciple must understand the importance of commitment, comprehend the value of spiritual maturation and the empowerment of Spirit-filled believers for daily service.

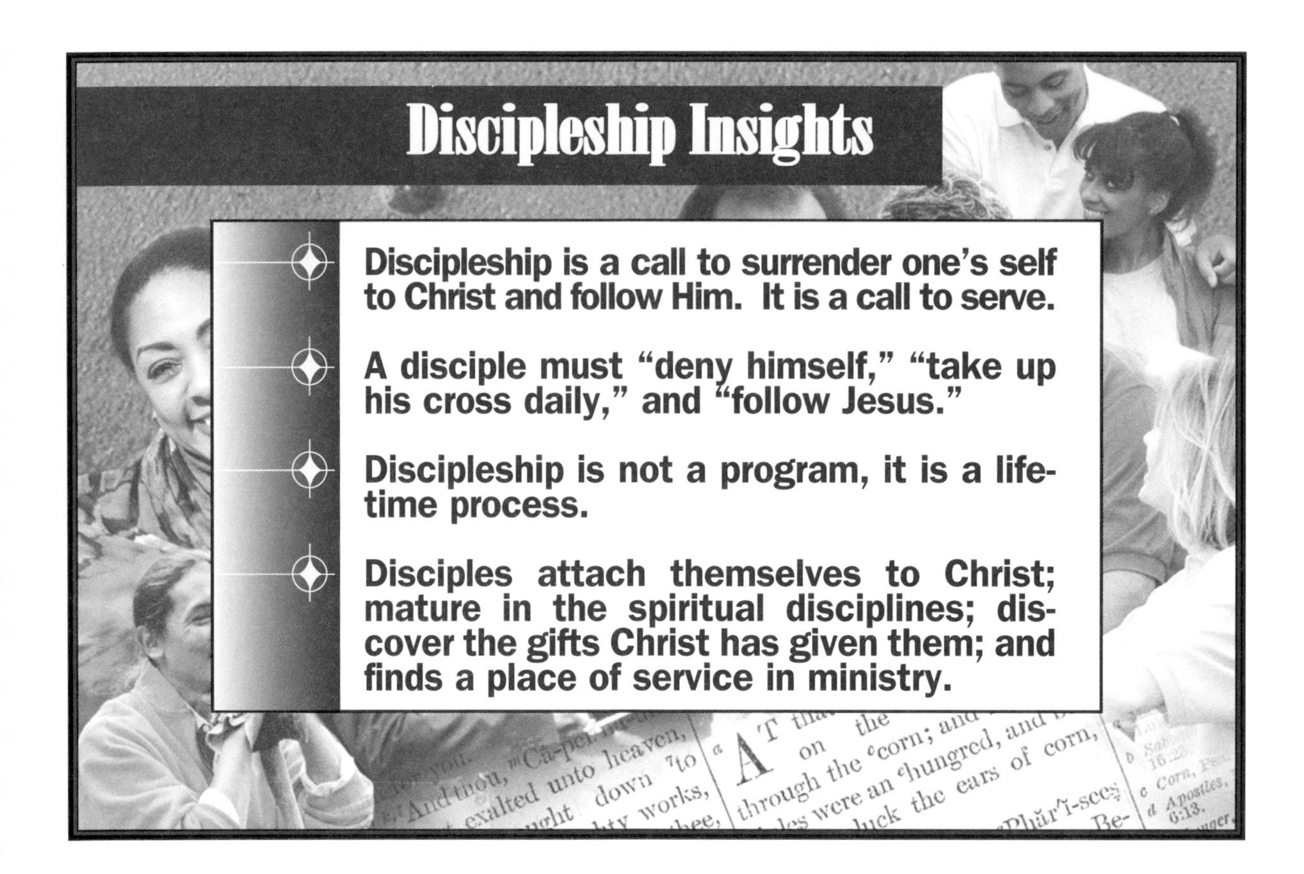

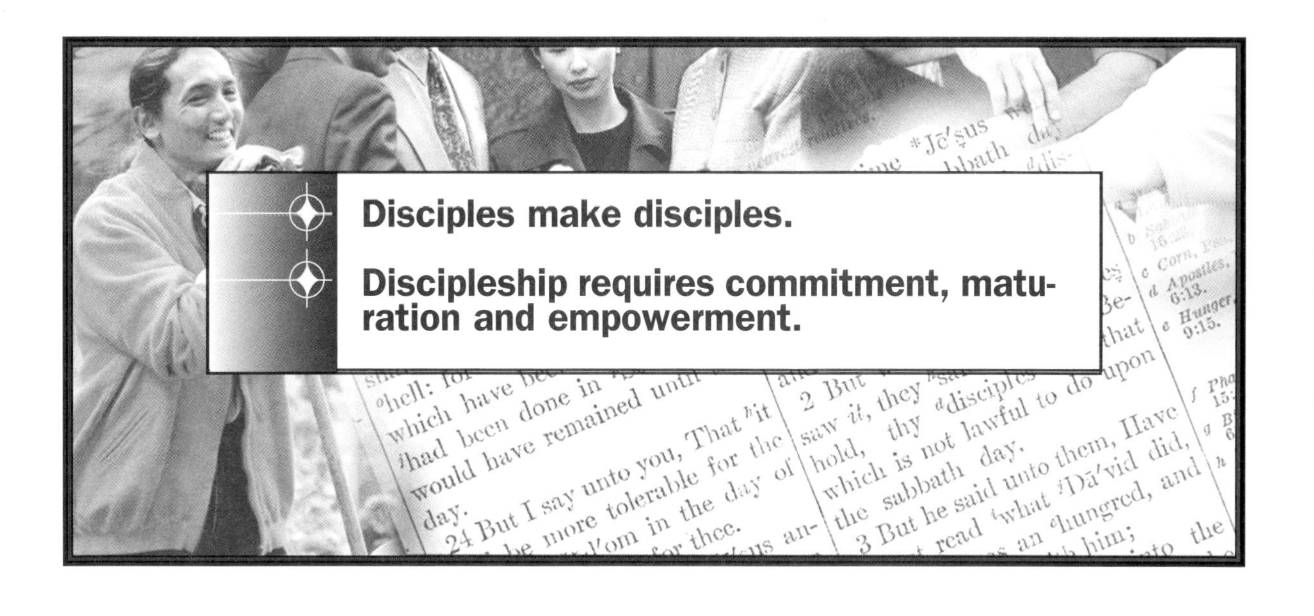

RESOURCES

Barclay, William. *The Gospel of Matthew*, Vol. 2, 2nd ed. Philadelphia: The Westminster Press, 1958.

Blackaby, Henry T., King, Claude V. *Experiencing God*. Nashville: Lifeway Press, 1990.

Briscoe, Stuart. *Discipleship for Ordinary People*. Wheaton: Harold Shaw Publishers, 1988.

Discipleship Journal (bimonthly). Navigators, Box 54470, Boulder, CO 80322.

Edgemon, Roy T., Williams, Steve J. *Leading Disciples In a Church*. Nashville: Convention Press, 1998.

Enrichment: A Journal for Pentecostal Ministry (Quarterly). The General Council of the Assemblies of God, 1445 Boonville, Springfield, MO 65802.

Hull, Bill. *The Disciple Making Pastor*. Tarrytown, New York: Fleming H. Revell Company, 1988.

Swindoll, Charles R. Discipleship: Ministry Up Close and Personal. Fulterton, CA: Charles R. Swindoll, 1990.

NOTES:

SALVATION

What Must I Do to Be Saved?

LESSON 2

Hoyt E. Stone

INTRODUCTION

The Meaning of Salvation

In today's world the term *salvation* is used broadly and perhaps carelessly. We read or hear of the salvation of someone's political career, the salvation of the British monarchy, or the salvation of some Fortune 500 company's bottom line as reflected on the New York Stock Exchange. All of which proves the word—meaning deliverance, pardon, reprieve, liberation, rescue, redemption—a useful tool of communication. It's important to note that in every nuance of meaning attributable to this word, there's the hint of trouble. Until or unless there is realization of trouble, or a problem, then there is no real meaning to the word *salvation*.

Our objective here is to apply this term *salvation* to the present human condition. Doing so demands understanding of where we are, an overview of possible causes, and a critique of viable solutions.

Good and Evil

Let's begin with a question—Why are things the way they are? Somewhere along the spectrum between the eternal optimists who claim "all is well with the world," and the proverbial pessimists who claim "everything is in a mess," most of us realistically bow to life's dilemma and note the ever-recurring tension between "good" and "evil." We shudder with the shock of man's inhumanity to man—crime, greed, moral outrage, degenerate lifestyles—and we glory in the grace and beauty of self-sacrificing goodness in the life of a Mother Teresa. We see shadows of both "good" and "evil" lurking in our own hearts and we keep asking why is this? Not only why is it happening, but also why can't we choose to stay with the best and the most noble of human aspirations rather than constantly swinging between opposite poles?

We are bombarded with rationalistic explanations for this life; but, even when the mind agrees, the heart continues in turmoil and there's a loneliness and a pain that human efforts never reach. It would be wonderful if we could simply conclude, "Well, that's just the way things are," and then live out our days in peace and contentment. It doesn't happen! Though we carefully craft all the pieces to the puzzle of life, they never make a whole. Something is always missing.

The Bible
His Holy Word

Since we as humans can't adequately explain nor in any true sense find a solution for the present human condition, it seems logical to look beyond ourselves and to heed God's revelation in the pages of His Holy Word, the Bible. Men and women have looked to the Bible for thousands of years. Within its pages they have discovered explanations that work and solutions that solve the problem. Otherwise, the Bible would have long ago become just another book either lost or relegated to the dustbin.

Human Condition

According to the Bible, the present human condition is the result of sin. Although carrying with it a litany of synonyms—transgression, offense, iniquity, error, vice, trespass—sin means rebellion. Things are the way they are because mankind is in rebellion against God the Creator. Ours is a total rebellion, a coup of the human heart in which we have dethroned God and elevated self. Ours is likewise a hopeless situation in that the heart gone astray cannot of itself save itself. The dilemma is described repeatedly throughout the pages of the Bible . . .

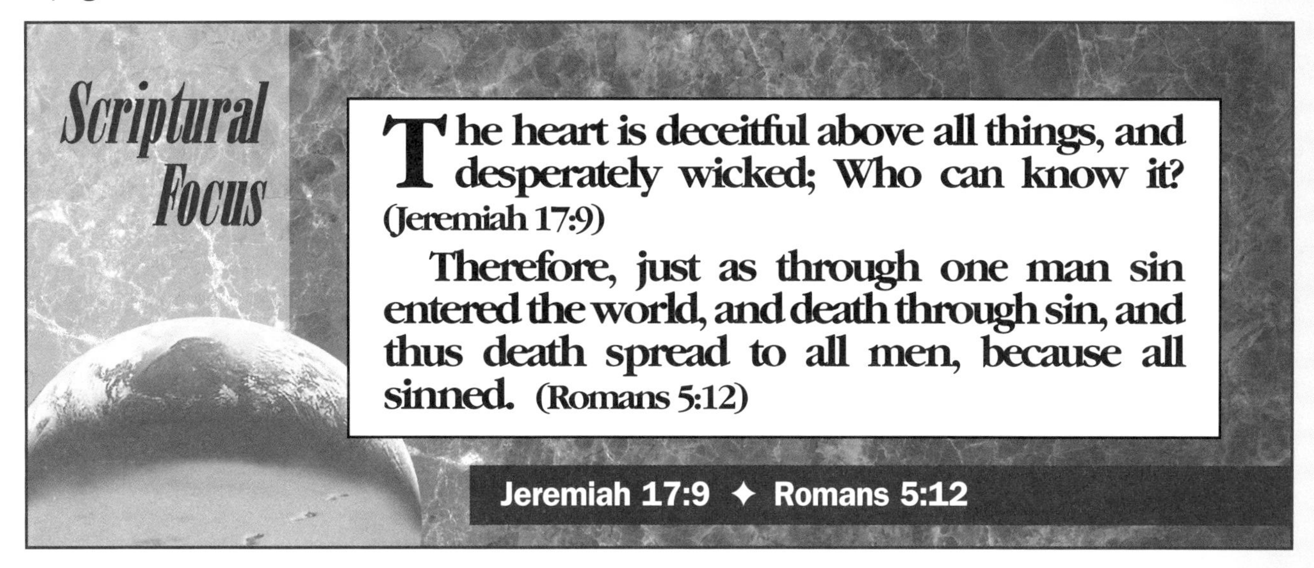

The Validity of the Bible

Should anyone question the validity of the Bible then let it be noted that Jesus predicated His claim for a church not on the mere words of the Bible but upon the living reality of those truths to be reflected in His disciples. That which the Bible claims can be, should be, and must be put to test in the marketplace of life. It must survive there or it will not survive at all.

Jesus Christ
Savior

Today, 2,000 years after His appearance in human flesh, followers of the lowly Nazarene preserve order and stability as salt in full strength (Matthew 5:13).

Christians permeate every facet of society, witnessing of Christ's power to redeem (Acts 1:8) and shining as beacons of hope in a world of darkness and despair (Matthew 5:14). These are not merely speculative ideas but truths that can be tested in the arena of life. Search for yourself: "Oh, taste and see that the Lord is good; blessed is the man who trusts in Him" (Psalm 34:8). Discover personally what God is doing in terms of life on Planet Earth and find in His Son, our Savior, real answers for the present and the future.

Psalm 34:8

GOD'S PROVISION

It's interesting to note how various New Testament writers introduced the message of salvation. The writer Luke addressed his remarks to a Gentile with little background or understanding of the Old Testament. He wrote, "It seemed good to me . . . to write to you an orderly account, most excellent Theophilus, that you may know the certainty of those things . . ." (Luke 1:3, 4).

Luke 1:3, 4

The author of Hebrews wrote to a Jewish audience who understood many truths from the Old Testament. He painted the background with a broad stroke, "God, who at various times and in various ways spoke in time past to the fathers by the prophets, has in these last days spoken to us by His Son, whom He has appointed heir of all things, through whom also He made the worlds; who being the brightness of His glory, and the express image of His person, and upholding all things by the word of His power, whom He had by Himself purged our sins, sat down at the right hand of the Majesty on high" (Hebrews 1:1-3).

Hebrews 1:1-3

God's Plan and Purpose

✦John 3:16

✦John 1:1-5

✦John 1:9-12

Yet it was John the Beloved who captured the grandeur and glory of God's plan and purpose. Not only did he give us the golden text of the Bible—"For God so loved the world, that He gave His only begotten Son, that whoever believes in Him should not perish but have everlasting life" (John 3:16)—but he also introduced his Gospel with, "In the beginning was the Word, and the Word was with God, and the Word was God. He was in the beginning with God. All things were made through Him; and without Him nothing was made that was made. In Him was life, and the life was the light of men. And the light shines in darkness, and the darkness did not comprehend it" (John 1:1-5); and zeroed in on the heart of the message with, "That [Jesus] was the true Light which gives light to every man coming into the world. He was in the world, and the world was made through Him, and the world did not know Him. He came to His own, and His own did not receive Him. But as many as received Him, to them He gave the right to become children of God, to those who believe in His name" (1:9-12).

The Gift of Salvation

Knowing man cannot save himself, the loving Father made provision through the sacrifice of His only begotten Son. Through Christ, God has chosen to rescue us, to liberate us, to pardon us, to grant a reprieve from our enslavement, to bring full and total deliverance. God grants to us the gift of salvation, full redemption, now and forever, based not on who we are or what we are, but solely on the atoning work of Christ.

Paul expresses it beautifully . . .

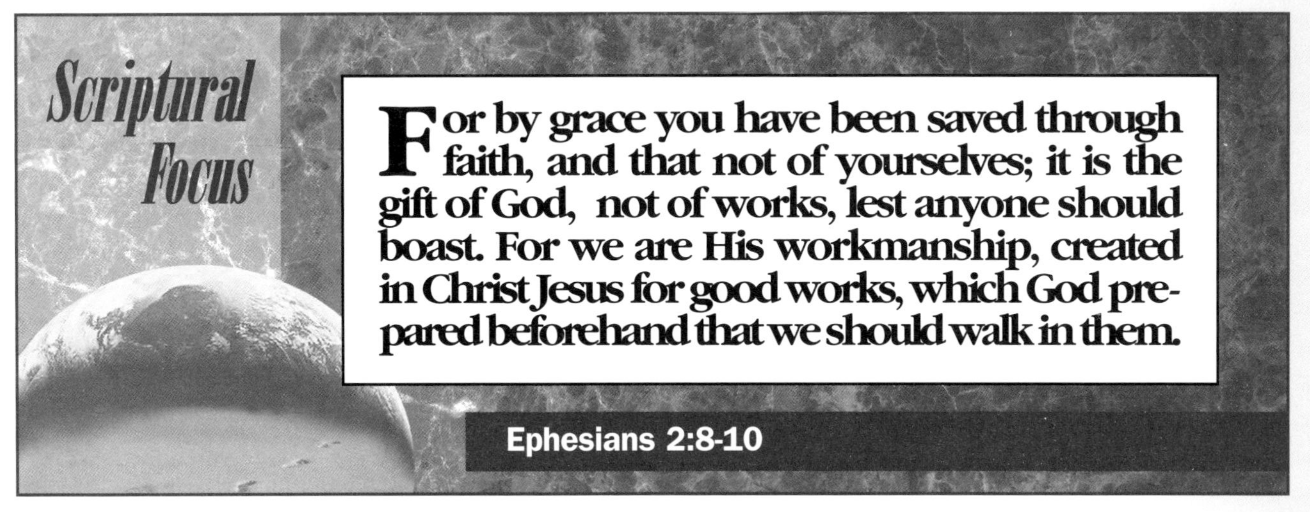

Applying the Truth

MY DAILY WALK WITH GOD

Meditating upon these thoughts, ask yourself these questions:

- Could it be that God really has provided a remedy for sin? ______________________________

____

- If so, would it not be foolish for me to ignore what He has done?______________________________

____

- What have I to lose by giving Him a chance in terms of my future?______________________________

____

____

- What other alternative is there? What am I supposed to do?

____

HUMAN RESPONSE

An Invitation

God's salvation message to the world, through Jesus Christ, is an invitation. It is an open invitation to every individual. Not only is this truth set forth in the announcement of Christ's mission to Mary—"for he shall save his people from their sins" (Matthew 1:21)—but it is stated repeatedly and with varying metaphors in Christ's own words . . .

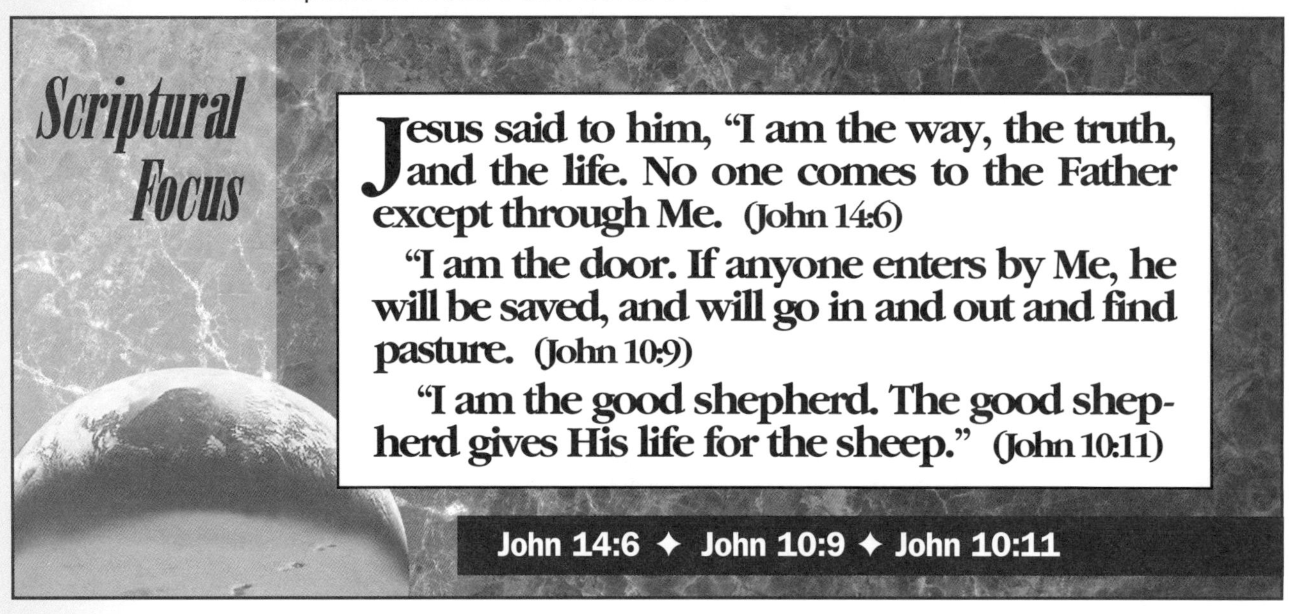

The Good News

The gospel message, the good news, proclaimed by the church always remains in essence an invitation. Jesus set this forth as a witnessing mandate when He promised the coming of His Holy Spirit—"But you shall receive power when the Holy Spirit has come upon you; and you shall be witnesses to Me in Jerusalem, and in all Judea and Samaria, and to the end of the earth" (Acts 1:8). He also incorporated the invitational aspects of the gospel in the Great Commission—"Go ye therefore, and teach all nations, baptizing them in the name of the Father, and of the Son, and of the Holy Ghost: Teaching them to observe all things whatsoever I have commanded you: and, lo, I am with you alway, even unto the end of the world" (Matthew 28:19, 20).

The Great Commission

Our Response

An invitation demands response. The gospel message demands response. Though free and purchased by the life's blood of God's own dear Son, salvation demands a response. God does not fence us in and force us to behave as animals. He created us with freedom to act and to choose. As the Psalmist noted, while each of us was "brought forth in iniquity" (Psalm 51:5) and born in sin—our genetic inheritance from the first man Adam—we have also, out of this free moral agency, chosen sin and rebellion. God did not restrict us in our choosing to sin, nor will He force us to accept His invitation. We each must freely choose, saying *yes* to His calling.

There are no draftees in God's kingdom, only volunteers. God's invitation goes forth to everyone.

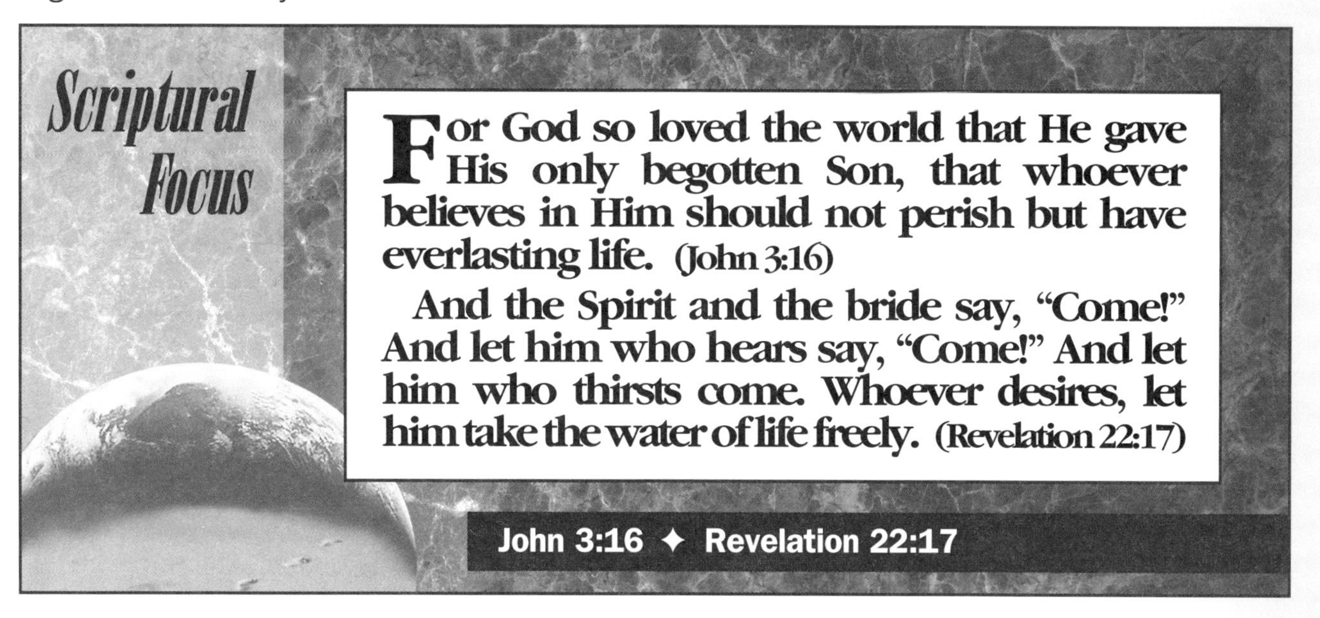

Say *Yes* to the Invitation

Those who accept the invitation, respond to the gospel, and say *yes* to God's grace and the beckoning Holy Spirit find life both now and in ages to come.

In Matthew's story of the rich young ruler we have an example of one who chose not to accept the invitation (Matthew 19:16-22). In Luke's Gospel we have an equally powerful story of a young son who first said no and then decided to reverse his decision and return to his father's house (Luke 15:11-24). Both stories illustrate in classic fashion the role our will plays in the drama of salvation. God has provided a redemptive lamb, His Son, but His invitation requires human response in faith to activate salvation's promise.

Respond in Faith

REPENTANCE

Life of Sin

Today, as always, the life of sin and rebellion offers certain fleshly pleasures and rewards. Many pursue their dreams on the broad road that leads to destruction. One of the great Scriptural references is made of young Moses who, "when he was come to years, refused to be called the son of Pharaoh's daughter; Choosing rather to suffer affliction with the people of God, than to enjoy the pleasures of sin for a season" (Hebrews 11:24, 25 KJV). The phrase to be noted here is "pleasures of sin for a season." Like all others, the season of sin and pleasure comes to an end. The way that seems right unto a man turns into the path that leads to death (Proverbs 16:25). Joy flees. Youth wanes. Happiness becomes a memory. Drugs and alcohol enslave. Lust and greed eat away at the soul. Hate and bitterness lead only to sorrow and pain. Where then does man turn? What power can save him?

The Meaning of Repentance

The Bible term which best describes the required human response to God's invitation is repentance. The word *repentance* commonly means sorrow, regret, remorse, contrition. As we use it here, it means recognition of spiritual bankruptcy, acknowledgment of failure and one's inability to cope. Repentance means turning from self and all human excuses and reaching out to God the Creator. It is changing of allegiance from a former master, sin and self, to a new master, Jesus Christ. Paul put it this way, "For with the heart one believes unto righteousness, and with the mouth confession is made unto salvation" (Romans 10:10).

Repentance means (1) recognition of sin, (2) contrition for sin, (3) confession of sin, and (4) forsaking of sin.

Applying the Truth

MY DAILY WALK WITH GOD

- Have you recognized your rebellion against God? ☐Yes ☐No
- Are you willing to confess and forsake your sins? ☐Yes ☐No
- Will you honestly and truly pray the following sinner's prayer?

Dear God, have mercy upon me, a sinner. Forgive my sins against my fellow man, my family, and most of all against You, my Creator. Grant me Your grace and pardon. Cleanse me through the redemptive blood of Your Son. Heal my broken heart and spirit. Give me peace. Lead me in paths of righteousness. Strengthen me with Your power and the presence of Your Holy Spirit. I thank You for Your Son Jesus Christ and I accept Jesus now, into my heart, as Lord and Master. Amen.

My response to this invitation________________________________

____

____

THE MIRACLE OF FAITH

Head Faith Transforms Into Heart Faith

The words of that prayer can be as meaningless as a quote from the morning newspaper. Or, they can be words of life. What they are to each of us as individuals will be determined by the miracle of faith. However one phrases the prayer, God demands only that it comes from the heart. His Spirit is present to make the words come alive as "head faith" transforms into "heart faith" and the Spirit bears witness to the living reality of Jesus Christ.

Some speak lightly of this whole concept of faith because they overlook the miracle involved. They tend to think Christian faith, saving faith, is similar to human faith. Human faith puts trust in physical evidence. Christian faith must reach beyond belief in the concrete and physical. It is absolute confidence in God through Jesus Christ and His work of salvation. Faith is depending on God's love and grace for salvation rather than on human rationalization. It is the miracle of faith that maintains total trust and dependence on God's leadership in the daily walk of life.

Christian Faith

REGENERATION

Regeneration
Being Born Again

Heartfelt, genuine repentance, followed by living faith produces the miracle of Christian conversion. It turns men and women around, as with Saul of Tarsus on the road to Damascus. It makes men and women willing to forsake all and follow Jesus, even to the giving of their lives in service to others.

The proper theological term for what happens in the life of a believer at this point is regeneration (Matthew 19:28; Titus 3:5). We also refer to this as being born again (John 3:1-20—the Lord's encounter with Nicodemus).

Herein lies the strength and the irrefutable proof of Christianity. When Jesus Christ was crucified, taken down from the cross and buried, His church existed only as a seed planted in the hearts of a few men and women. The Bible clearly chronicles their despair, disappointment, and loss of faith. Then came Easter morning! Then came the Resurrection! Then came the Lord's personal appearance to those disciples and they were born again. Those same disciples, at the Lord's instruction, gathered in the Upper Room in Jerusalem and received the outpouring of the Holy Spirit. In the power of that Spirit they experienced a new life that quite literally changed the world.

Experiencing New Life

NEW LIFE

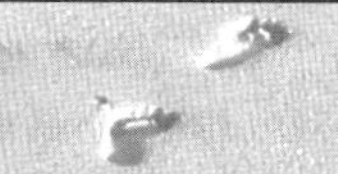

Faith, Hope, and Assurance

For nearly 2,000 years we have continuing testimonies of men and women transformed, regenerated, born again through personal confrontation with the resurrected, living Christ. It is this new life in Christ that provides the cutting edge of the gospel. It is this new life in Christ that enables every believer to step forth in faith, with hope in the heart, and with an assurance of salvation that no tragedy or setback in life can obliterate.

A New Creation

✦ 2 Corinthians 5:17

This new life in Christ is what Paul wrote to the Corinthians about when he stated, "Therefore, if anyone is in Christ, he is a new creation; old things have passed away; behold, all things have become new" (2 Corinthians 5:17). He told his Galatian brethren that his Jewishness was not important, "For in Christ

♦ Galatians 6:15

♦ Ephesians 4:22-24

Jesus neither circumcision nor uncircumcision avails anything, but a new creation" (Galatians 6:15). And he reminded the Ephesians, "That you put off, concerning your former conduct, the old man which grows corrupt according to the deceitful lusts, and be renewed in the spirit of your mind, and that you put on the new man which was created according to God, in true righteousness and holiness" (Ephesians 4:22-24).

Applying the Truth

MY DAILY WALK WITH GOD

Head knowledge becomes living faith through a direct confrontation with Jesus Christ, as witnessed and made real through the Holy Spirit. Has this happened in your heart?____

____

____

Signs of regeneration are seen in the desire to live differently, to change, to forsake the old ways and become a new creature in Christ. What is happening in your life at the moment?_____

____

____

Recognize that new life and a new loyalty (to Christ and His church) requires both the human will and the determination to see things changed. Seek Him for guidance and strength.

LESSON REVIEW

Divine salvation is the only solution for our world. The human condition is such that men and women cannot save themselves, no matter how hard they try. Nor can rational men and women deny the reality of society's terrible plight and need for redemption. God has provided a solution in the redemptive gift of His Son Jesus Christ. He requires only that men and women hear the good news, believe in their hearts that God has raised Him from the dead, repent of their sins and accept Christ as Lord and Master.

With repentance comes the miracle of faith, and with this living faith comes regeneration and new life through the Holy Spirit. It is this new life exemplified in the daily walk and daily talk of believers that draws others to Christ. This new life also prepares the church for the coming new world restored in power and majesty when Christ as Lord shall reign forever and ever. Amen.

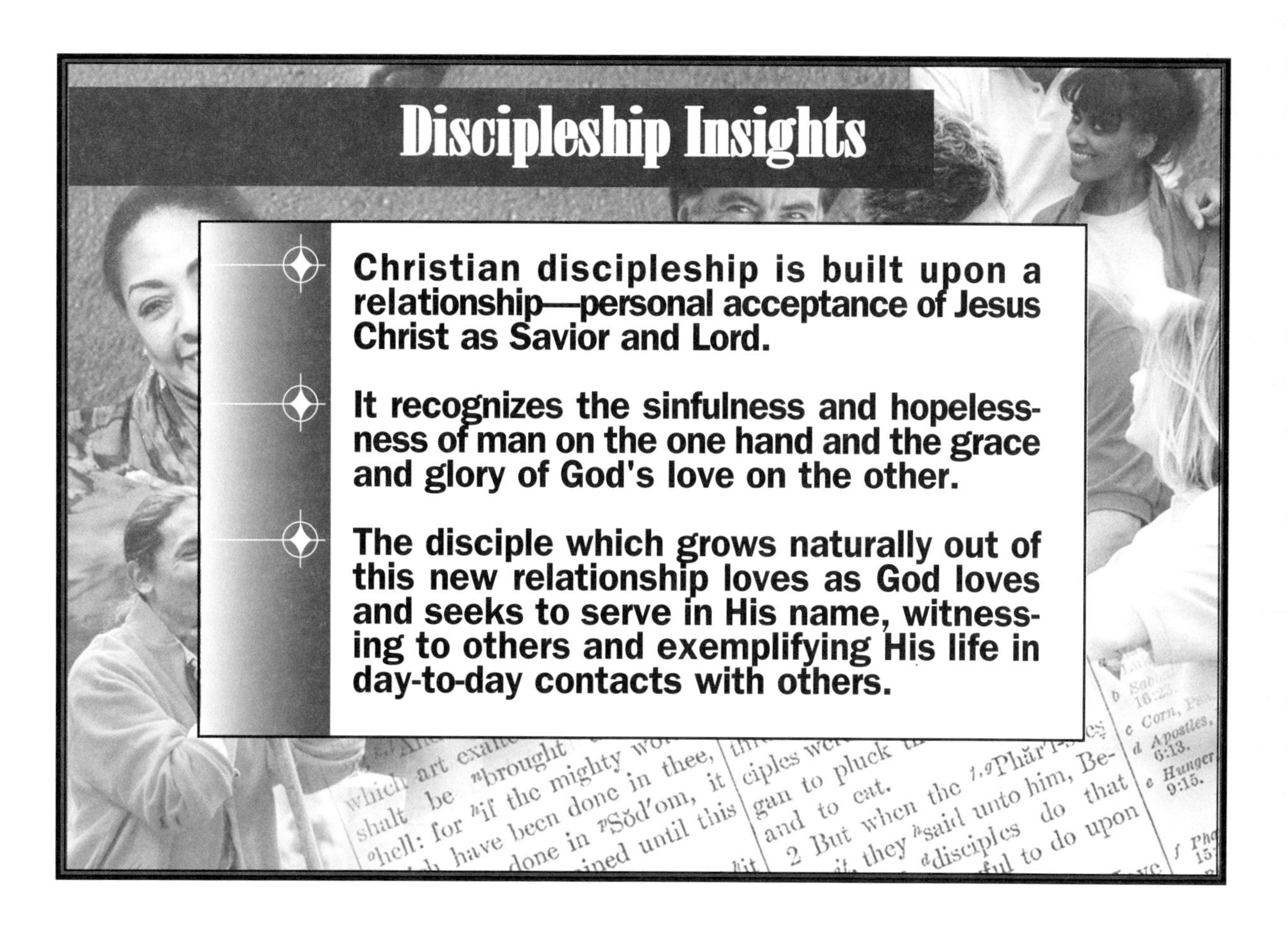

NOTES:____

BIBLE

BIBLE

God's Written Revelation

3
LESSON

Ken Bell

INTRODUCTION

The Bible is referred to in many different ways. It is sometimes called the Word of God, the Good Book, the Holy Scriptures or the Sword of the Spirit. It is also known as the Book of books and the living Word. Some call it simply THE Book. Whatever name is ascribed to it, it towers above all other writings.

The Bible *Miraculous*

This is true for a number of reasons:

1. It is miraculous in its origin—coming to us by divine inspiration.
2. It is miraculous in its durability—outlasting the opposition of its critics and surviving the attempts of its enemies to exterminate it.
3. It is miraculous in its results—transforming the lives of those that read and believe it.
4. It is miraculous in its harmony—agreeing in all its parts, even though it is a collection of 66 books written over a period of approximately 1600 years by about 40 different authors.
5. It is miraculous in its message—telling of many occasions when God supernaturally intervened in the affairs of men to accomplish His redemptive purposes.
6. It is miraculous in its preservation—maintaining its accuracy and reliability down through the centuries.

The Bible *Most Influential*

In fact the Bible is the world's best-known and most influential book. To refer to the Bible as "the Word of God" or "Holy Scriptures" is really a confession of faith. Non-Christian religions also have "scriptures"—documents that these groups consider sacred and authoritative. For example, the Hindus cherish the

Vedas, the *Upanishads*, and the *Bhagavadgita*; the Buddhists venerate the recorded teachings of Buddha; and the followers of Islam revere the *Koran*. The three great world religions—Christianity, Judaism, and Islam—all claim the Old Testament's authority for their beliefs. Christianity also accepts the New Testament as authoritative. So, the Christian Bible consists of both the Old Testament and the New Testament.

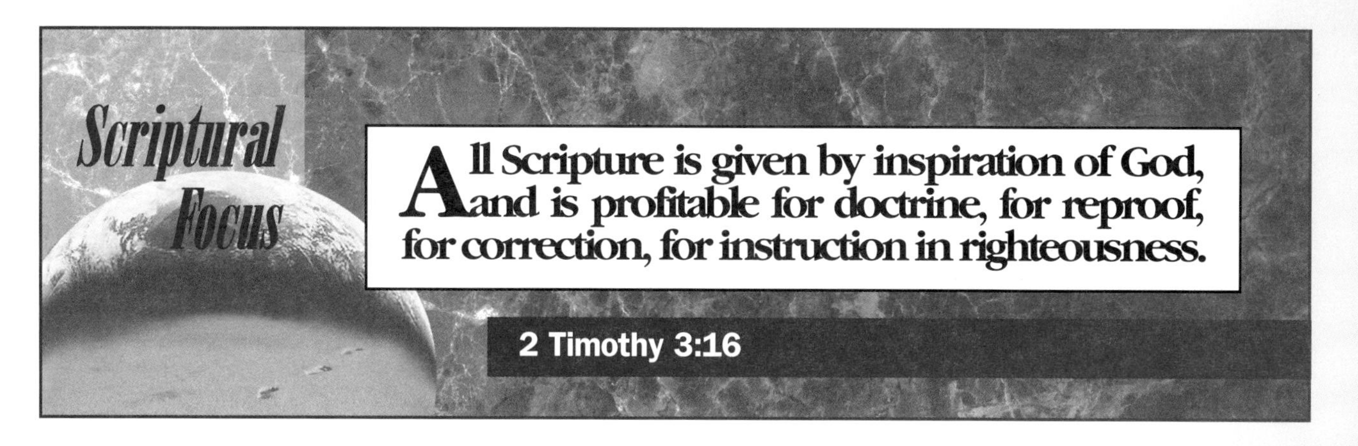

BACKGROUND INFORMATION

The word "Bible" is not found in the Biblical text itself. It is through the Latin term *biblia*, which means, "book," that the English term "Bible" derived.

The Bible is a collection of 66 books and is composed of the Old Testament, consisting of 39 books and the New Testament consisting of 27 books. These books are divided into 1,189 chapters and 31,173 verses. The Old Testament is much longer and more diverse than the New Testament and is often referred to as the Hebrew or Jewish Bible. It records the history of the Jewish people's relationship with God.

Old Testament
39 Books

New Testament
27 Books

The Bible should not be understood as an anthology of stories gathered together over a period of time, nor should it be viewed as just a collection of religious writings brought together in a haphazard manner. It is a history with a purpose. It is *His-story*. It has been called "salvation history" or "faith history," because it records the historic acts of God in redeeming mankind. It is this theme which provides the unity of all 66 books, because each contributes in its own way to the theme of God redeeming man. The Old Testament makes more sense when read in light of the New Testament, and the New Testament is richer and more meaningful when read as the complement—not just supplement—of the Old Testament.

The Bible is a letter from God with one personal address on it.

—Soren Kierkegard

THE IDEA OF COVENANT

Old and New Testament

Although the two divisions of the Bible are called testaments, the main idea of each division is covenant. The term *covenant* refers to an agreement between two parties—in this case, between God and man. The Old Testament, then, is the record of the old covenant, the covenant God made with the Jews at Mt. Sinai. The New Testament is the record of the new covenant that Christ made in His blood. This idea of covenant is extremely important in understanding the message and meaning of the Scriptures. The covenant God made with Israel at Mt. Sinai delineated certain responsibilities and purposes they were to fulfill as a nation if they were to be God's chosen people. Israel did not live up to that covenant. Under the inspiration of the Holy Spirit, Jeremiah prophesied of a new covenant God would make with His people that was to be an inner and spiritual covenant (Jeremiah 31:31ff.). Christ established this new covenant with His life, death and resurrection. All who accept this new covenant—Christians—constitute the New Israel. So, the old covenant finds its highest significance and "reason for being" in the new covenant.

THE INSPIRATION OF THE BIBLE

Because the Bible has been with us for so long, it is easy for us to take the Bible and its process of development for granted. It can be helpful to understand a little bit about the complex and laborious way in which the Bible was transmitted from the mind of God to the printed page we are so familiar with today.

God's Written Revelation

Long before there was a Bible, God communicated with man by means of angels, visions, dreams, or other forms of direct communication. But as the population of man increased, so did the need for a written record of God's revelation to man. To supply this need, God inspired holy men to write the Scriptures. ". . . for prophecy never came by the will of man, but holy men of God spoke as they were moved by the Holy Spirit" (2 Peter 1:21).

God Inspired

2 Timothy 3:16 declares: "All Scripture is given by inspiration of God, and is profitable for doctrine, for reproof, for correction, for instruction in righteousness." The word "inspiration" comes from the Greek word *theopneustos*, which means "God-breathed." Through this process of inbreathing the mind of God was communicated to human authors. Utilizing words from the writers' own vocabularies and their own unique styles, the Holy Spirit guided and directed the writing of every word in the Bible. Only the Bible contains all doctrinal and ethical truth God has revealed to us. Only the Bible is the complete and final revelation of God for the faith and practice of believers. Every spirit or prophet who claims a new or different revelation is not of God. Only the Bible has been confirmed by Christ to be God's infallible Word.

Applying the Truth

MY DAILY WALK WITH GOD

What Does the Bible Really Say?
(True or False)
Which of the following statements are Biblical quotations?

____ 1. "Cleanliness is next to godliness."

____ 2. "God helps those who help themselves."

____ 3. "An honest confession is good for the soul."

____ 4. "We are as prone to sin as sparks fly upward."

____ 5. "Money is the root of all evil."

____ 6. "Honesty is the best policy."

The answer? While some of these statements are truisms, none of them, as quoted, are found in the Bible! So before you quote the Bible, make sure it is in the Bible.

UNDERSTANDING THE BIBLE

Barriers to Understanding

Why can't we just immediately and spontaneously understand the Bible when we read it? There are several barriers to a spontaneous understanding of Scripture. First of all, there is the historical gap in time from the original writers and those reading Scripture today. Not understanding the historical context in which a passage of Scripture is written can lead to an incorrect interpretation of the meaning in contemporary society. For example, one can easily understand Jonah's reluctance to preach to the Ninevites when one understands the extreme cruelty and sinfulness of the people of Ninevah.

✦ Historical Gap in Time

A second barrier to a spontaneous understanding of the Bible is the cultural difference between the Hebrews and our culture today. It's like our being in a goldfish bowl (our culture and time) looking at another goldfish bowl (Biblical times and culture). Failure to understand and recognize these differences can also lead to a misunderstanding of what the Bible is really saying.

✦ Cultural Differences

A third barrier to a spontaneous understanding of Scripture has to do with the linguistic differences. The Bible was written in three different languages—Hebrew, Aramaic and Greek. Each of these languages has idioms and figures of speech which are different from English. The translation of Scripture from these languages to English often obscures the author's intended meanings.

✦ Linguistic Differences

The fourth and final barrier to a spontaneous understanding of the Bible is

✦ Philosophical Differences

the philosophical difference between the authors of the Bible and us today. Every person views the world through their own perspective. To fail to acknowledge that the Biblical authors' worldviews may be much different from our own will lead to a misinterpretation or misapplication of the text.

Despite these barriers to a quick and accurate understanding of the Bible, the new Christian must not be discouraged in reading the Word of God. Many find it difficult to read because they read it as they would read any other book, and it is not the same as any other book. God the Father is the giver of Holy Scripture; God the Son is the theme of Holy Scripture; and God the Holy Spirit is the author, authenticator and interpreter of Holy Scripture. The Holy Spirit will illuminate the meaning of a passage to the sincere reader.

THE OLD TESTAMENT

A Canon

Not only was the Holy Spirit involved in the process of the inspiration and writing down of the Scriptures, but was also active in its preservation and transmission. In religious usage, a *canon* is the official list of books that a religious community judges to be its authoritative source of doctrinal and ethical belief. We believe that we have the complete canon of Scripture that God intended for us to have.

Old Testament Divisions

Perhaps the most popular division of the Old Testament among Protestants is:

- **The Law** (5 books)—*Genesis, Exodus, Leviticus, Numbers, and Deuteronomy*

- **The Historical Books** (12 books)—*Joshua, Judges, Ruth, 1 & 2 Samuel, 1 & 2 Kings, 1 & 2 Chronicles, Ezra, Nehemiah, and Esther*

- **The Poetical Books** (6 books)—*Job, Psalms, Proverbs, Ecclesiastes, Song of Solomon, and Lamentations*

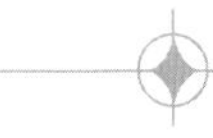

- **The Major Prophets** (4 books)—*Isaiah, Jeremiah, Ezekiel, and Daniel*

- **The Minor Prophets** (12 books)—*Hosea, Joel, Amos, Obadiah, Jonah, Micah, Nahum, Habakkuk, Zephaniah, Haggai, Zechariah, and Malachi*

Languages

Hebrew is the language of the Old Testament except a portion (Daniel 2:4-7:28; Ezra 4:8-6:18; 7:12-26; and Jeremiah 10:11) written in Aramaic. Aramaic occurs in books that have their setting in the period when the Jews were exiled from their land. From the seventh century BC on, it was the official court language of the Babylonian and the Persian empires.

Manuscripts

Most of the *autographs* (original manuscripts) of the Old Testament were probably written on papyrus (a paper-like material for writing). To our knowledge none of the original manuscripts (*autographs*) exist today. The oldest copies of the Bible were made from other copies of the original. Some of the oldest copies of Old Testament manuscripts were found in the Essene community at Qumran, Israel and are referred to as the Dead Sea Scrolls.

Without the Old Testament, we would have no information about the origin of the universe, the origin of man, the beginnings of sin, the birth and growth of the Hebrew nation, or the purposes of God for the world. An understanding of the Old Testament is absolutely necessary if we are to interpret the New Testament faithfully and accurately.

The Septuagint

The New Testament was never intended to replace the Old Testament. At the time of Jesus and His followers, the Old Testament was the only written authority for both Jews and Christians. When the New Testament writers refer to "Scripture" or "the Law and the Prophets" they mean the Hebrew Bible, although they commonly use a Greek translation of the Hebrew text known as the *Septuagint*. The *Septuagint* was a Greek translation of the Hebrew Bible that had been published in Alexandria, Egypt, during the last two centuries BC. This version became the standard Biblical text for Greek-speaking Jews scattered throughout the Greco-Roman world.

Christians cite various reasons for not reading the Old Testament. "The Old Testament applied to the Jews and is irrelevant for Christians." "I can't understand the Old Testament." "Reading the Old Testament is boring and puts me to sleep." But, it is a serious mistake to view the Old Testament as outdated and no longer useful. Without the Old Testament the New Testament would be a mystery and open to speculation. The Old Testament can be understood and appreciated if the time is taken to study it with an open heart and mind.

Value of the Old Testament

The value of the Old Testament books for modern man is that they inspire hope in those who read them. The words and works of God during the Old Testament age, the victories men won, the defeats they suffered, all serve to fill our hearts with hope as they reveal the path to victory and the road to judgment. We can experience conviction from the indictments against sin. We can learn what is pleasing to God from its laws and counsel. We can be encouraged by the psalms of prayer and praise. We can gain perspective on the acts of God throughout history in redeeming mankind. From the Old Testament, we can understand more about the character of Christ's millennial kingdom.

Begin your study of the Old Testament with the following presuppositions:

- As to origin, the Old Testament is the inspired word of God written through holy men of old.
- As to history, the Old Testament is both accurate and faithful in its presentation.
- As to religion, the Old Testament is a foreshadowing of the ultimate revelation of God in His Son, Jesus Christ.
- As to value, the Old Testament is vital for a proper and correct understanding of the New Testament.

It is extremely important that the Old Testament not be treated as words or history, but that as the Word, it becomes flesh in our lives.

Applying the Truth
MY DAILY WALK WITH GOD

Some Say: Everyone is basically good.
THE BIBLE SAYS: "All have sinned" (Romans 3:23).

Some Say: There is no hell, so there's no need to be concerned.
THE BIBLE SAYS: "Fear him who . . . has power to throw you into hell" (Luke 12:5).

Some Say: Heaven is not a real place.
THE BIBLE SAYS: "I am going . . . to prepare a place for you" (John 14:2).

Some Say: There is no such thing as life after death.
THE BIBLE SAYS: "Man is destined to die . . . and after that . . . judgment" (Hebrews 9:27).

Some Say: We can do nothing about the future. What is going to be will be.
THE BIBLE SAYS: "You must be born again" (John 3:7). How can you be born again? "Whoever confesses and renounces [his sins] finds mercy" (Proverbs 28:13). "To all who received him [Christ] . . . he gave the right to become children of God" (John 1:12).

Some Say: We cannot be sure of salvation or our destiny when we die.
THE BIBLE SAYS: "You may know that you have eternal life" (1 John 5:13).

It is extremely important early in your Christian experience to decide you will trust what the Bible says over what someone else may tell you. "Let God be true and every man a liar . . . " (Romans 3:4).

THE NEW TESTAMENT

New Testament Canon

Each of the 27 books of the New Testament originated as a separate document and at first circulated independently of the others. Paul's letters, for example, were sent individually to different small Christian groups in Greece and Asia Minor. About 90 AD, some unknown person searched the archives of the various Pauline churches for surviving copies of the apostle's correspondence, gathering them together in a single unit. This anonymous Pauline disciple began a collection to which the Gospels, Acts, and other documents gradually were added creating a New Testament canon. Canonization was not, however, the result of any act or decree of the church.

Athanasius

The first official listing of the 27 books that accords with our present listing was not issued until 367 AD. It appeared in the Easter Letter of Athanasius, bishop of Alexandria. Athanasius cited only the 27 books as authoritative.

The New Testament was written in the same kind of *koine* (common) Greek as the Septuagint. Most of the 27 books of the New Testament were composed during the half-century between circa 50 and 100 AD. The oldest surviving Christian writings are copies of the letters of Paul, written between 50 and 62 AD.

New Testament Categories

The New Testament contains several different categories of literature. The contents are not arranged chronologically but according to four literary classifications.

A. GOSPELS

✦ Gospels

The term gospel translates the Greek word *euangelion* (good news). The Gospels—Matthew, Mark, Luke, John—tell the story of Jesus' ministry, death and resurrection. The term *Evangelist* refers to the writer of an *euangelion* (Gospel). The only literary genre the early Christians invented, the gospel is a narrative—a story—about Jesus' deeds and teachings. The Gospels do not attempt to present a complete life of Jesus or to explain what forces—social, psychological, cultural, historical, or political—impacted on His life and ministry. Only two of the Gospels—Matthew and Luke—include information about Jesus' birth and infancy. None gives even a scrap of information about his formative years, education, associations, or any other experience that a modern historian would regard as essential. Luke records a single incident of Jesus' youth, a pilgrimage from Nazareth to Jerusalem (Luke 2:22-40). The Gospels tell us nothing about what happened to Jesus between the ages of 12 and about 30 except for what is recorded in Luke 2:52: “And Jesus increased in wisdom and stature, and in favour with God and man.”

All four concentrate exclusively on the last phase of His life. Only the final week of Jesus' life is related in detail—the events leading up to His arrest, trial, and crucifixion known as the Passion (suffering and death of Jesus).

B. A HISTORY OF THE EARLY CHURCH

✦ History of Early Church

The Book of Acts continues the story of Christianity's origins, written by Luke the author of the Gospel of Luke.

C. LETTERS OR EPISTLES

✦ Letters or Epistles

After the gospel and history forms comes a collection of 21 letters or epistles. The first set of letters is by Paul, others are by Pauline disciples, and others are attributed to other early Christian leaders.

✦**Study of End Times**

D. APOCALYPSE

The Book of Revelation represents the fourth and final literary form of the New Testament. The title Revelation translates the Greek word *apokalypsis*, which means an "uncovering" or "unveiling." Its primary focus is eschatology, which is a study of the end times.

The New Testament is the primary source for the Christian faith. It describes the new covenant between God and man, which is not based on man's works, but on grace and faith. It is extremely important for the new Christian to read and study the New Testament.

HOW TO STUDY THE BIBLE

The Bible is the only thing that can combat the devil. Quote the scriptures and the devil will run . . . use the scriptures like a sword and you'll drive temptation away.
—Billy Graham

How much time does it take to read from Genesis to Revelation? Reading slow enough to be heard and understood, the total reading time is about 72 hours. If that time is broken down into minutes and divided into 365 days, a person could read through the Bible, cover to cover, in about 12 minutes a day.

Martin Luther said he studied his Bible like he gathered apples. First he shook the whole tree, that the ripest might fall; then he shook each limb, and when he had shaken each limb, he shook each branch, and after each branch, every twig; and then he looked under every leaf.

Search the Bible as a whole, shaking the whole tree. Read it rapidly, as you would any other book. Then shake every limb—study book after book. Then shake every branch, giving attention to the chapters when they do not break the sense. Then shake each twig, by a careful study of the paragraphs and sentences. And you will be rewarded if you will look under each leaf, by searching the meaning of the words.

CONCLUSION

Know the Bible

One of the greatest problems in the church today is the neglect of reading the Bible. Many believers remain weak because they fail to read the Bible and assimilate helpful passages from the Word of God. In times of stress, sorrow, or temptation, the Holy Spirit can bring those portions to their remembrance to comfort, warn, and direct them. The psalmist declares, "Your word I have hidden in my heart, That I might not sin against You" (Psalm 119:11).

The followers of some pagan religions are often required to saturate their minds with their sacred writings. For instance, no one can teach in a Mohammedan mosque until he has first memorized the entire Koran! One missionary tells that for 21 hours she heard a group of Buddhist priests quoting their devotional literature from memory, seldom if ever making a mistake.

Today cults and "isms"are leading many astray, because they don't recognize how they are being deceived. The only way to prevent this is to be indoctrinated with the truth so we will be much more discerning. For example, if a person is solidly grounded in the teaching of salvation by grace, he will not swallow the line of the legalists who inject human works into the matter of being saved. If he is well instructed about the person of Christ, he won't accept the error of those who deny the Savior's deity. Knowing the truth of the Second Coming of Jesus, he will not be swayed by those who distort the blessed hope, making it something less than the personal, bodily return of the Lord. A thorough knowledge of essential Biblical doctrines is the only way to detect counterfeits!

LESSON REVIEW

- Why is the Bible considered to be a miraculous book?__________

____

____

____

- What scriptural text is used as a basis for the doctrine of inspiration?

____

- What are four barriers to a spontaneous understanding of Scripture?______________________________________

____

____

____

- List the books of the Old Testament in the order in which they appear in our Bible.________________________________

____

____

____

____

____

List the books of the New Testament in the order in which they appear in our Bible.____________________________________

____

____

____

____

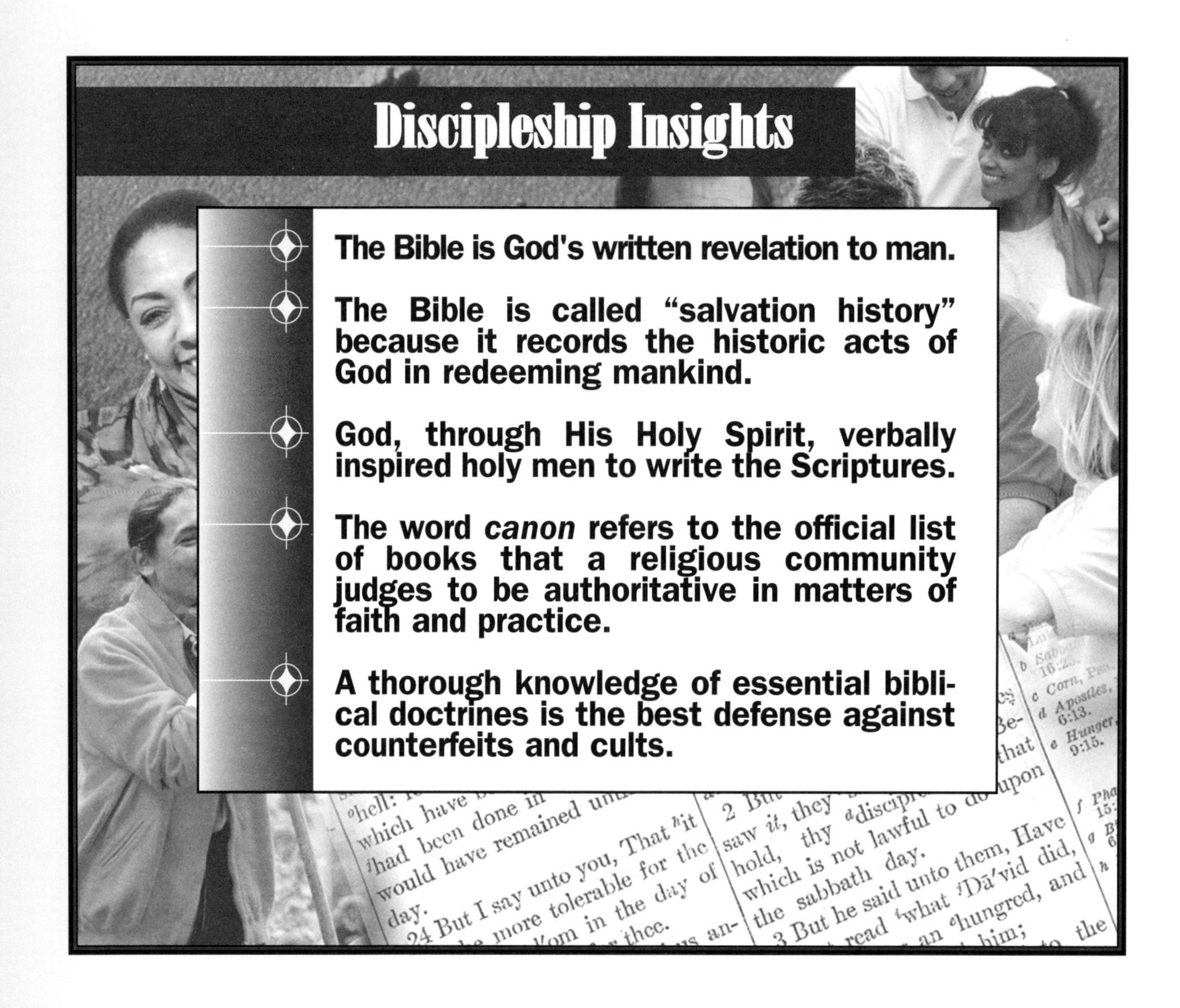

RESOURCES

Allison, Joseph D. *Bible Study Resource Guide*. Nashville, Tennessee: Thomas Nelson, 1982.

Brooks, D.P. *The Bible: How to Understand and Teach It*. Nashville, Tennessee: Broadman Press, 1969.

Conn, Charles W. *The Bible: Book of Books*. Cleveland, Tennessee: Pathway Press.

Geisler, Norman L. *A Popular Survey of the Old Testament*. Grand Rapids, Michigan: Baker, 1977.

Smith, Bob. *Basics of Bible Interpretation*. Waco, Texas: Word, 1978.

Stevens, William W. *A Guide for New Testament Study*. Nashville, Tennessee: Broadman Press, 1977.

NOTES:

PRAYER

Talking With God

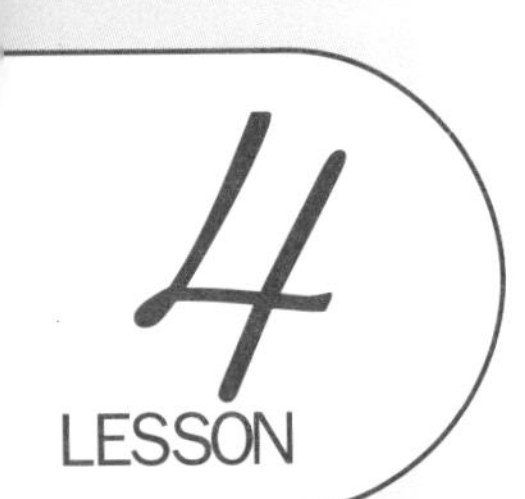

Lucille Walker

INTRODUCTION

You Accepted Christ

When you accepted Christ as your personal Savior, you "asked" Him to come into your heart. You "talked" with God, confessing your sins and you "spoke" with Him the same way you might "converse" with a family member, teacher, minister or friend.

All the action verbs listed above demonstrate the most intimate and life-changing aspects of your relationship with God: prayer. It is the practice and regularly-scheduled private time of prayer, this "conversation" with the Lord, that will take you to the next level of your spiritual relationship. Prayer is God's gift to us.

Let us become better acquainted with this gift of God called prayer. Right now, pause, pray, and give thanks for:

Entering into His Presence

- The power of prayer to take us into the presence of God by the name of Jesus;
- New birth here and now by the blood of Jesus;
- Forgiveness of sins, acceptance and eternal life forever with God;
- Family members, friends and others who need to make this discovery.

Prayer is Scriptural. Consider this instructional passage on prayer . . .

And when you pray, you shall not be like the hypocrites. For they love to pray standing in the synagogues and on the corners of the streets, that they may be seen by men. Assuredly, I say to you, they have their reward. But you, when you pray, go into your room, and when you have shut your door, pray to your Father who is in the secret place; and your Father who sees in secret will reward you openly.

Matthew 6:5, 6

Consider other passages:

- Men always ought to pray (Luke 18:1).
- And seek the peace of the city where I have caused you to be carried away captive, and pray to the Lord for it; for in its peace you will have peace (Jeremiah 29:7).
- But when you pray . . . (Matthew 6:7).
- Jesus said . . . "ask the Father in my name" (John 16:23).
- Ask and you will receive (John 16:24).
- Pray without ceasing (1 Thessalonians 5:17).
- Call to me and I will show you great and mighty things, which you do not know (Jeremiah 33:3).
- If my people, who are called by my name, will humble themselves, and pray and seek my face, and turn from their wicked ways, then I will hear from heaven, and will forgive their sin and heal their land (2 Chronicles 7:14).

Major chapters to read: 1 Kings 8, 9; 2 Chronicles 20; Daniel 9; Ezra 9; Nehemiah 9; Matthew 6; Luke 11; Ephesians 6.

PRAYER IS UNIVERSAL: EVERYONE CAN PRAY

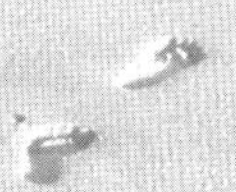

Prayer is a progression in your spiritual journey. As you progress and mature in your Christianity, so should your prayer life. The more you practice the easier and more effective it becomes.

Prayer Is Progressive

Prayer can be like traveling. At first, you crawl, then you take one step at a time. Before you realize it you are traveling over oceans and into continents, on to interceding for the nations.

A Biblical Example of Prayer

Take for example the Biblical figure Samuel, whose mother, Hannah, gave him to the service of God after he was weaned. Read about him in the book of 1 Samuel 1-3. Eli, the priest, had to explain to Samuel that it was the voice of God calling to him and Eli instructed Samuel: "Go lie down; and it shall be, if He calls you, that you must say, 'Speak, Lord, for Your servant hears'" (1 Samuel 3:9).

Learning to Pray

Probably the greatest thing a Christian can do is pray. The most important lesson we can learn is how to pray. Nothing is more essential but often it is most neglected. If we learn to pray more effectively, we will be able to release God's power for our personal needs and the needs of others. The apostle James said "You do not have because you do not ask" (James 4:2).

God wants us to be partners with Him in prayer. Prayer was a very important part of Jesus' ministry while He was here on earth in His incarnation. Prayer is now the main work of Jesus as He sits at the right hand of God makes intercession for us (Romans 8:34). The writer of Hebrews says, "He is able to save to the uttermost those who come to God through Him, since He ever lives to make intercession for them" (Hebrews 7:25).

Prayer and the Holy Spirit

Prayer is also one of the main ministries of the Holy Spirit - the Advocate, the Comforter, the Helper. Paul declared in scripture, "Likewise, the Spirit also helps in our weaknesses. For we do not know what we should pray for as we ought, but the Spirit Himself makes intercession for us with groanings which cannot be uttered. Now He who searches the hearts knows what the mind of the Spirit is, because he makes intercession for the saints according to the will of God" (Romans 8:26-27).

WHAT IS PRAYER?

Prayer is Recognition of God

Prayer is first recognizing that God is. Then, it is coming into His presence in repentance, confessing our sins and our need of Him. Prayer is humbling ourselves in worship of the holy God of Heaven, our Creator, our Father and accepting His loving forgiveness. Prayer is acknowledging God, talking with Him and listening. Prayer is praising God and loving Him for all He has done for us. Prayer also includes obeying God and waiting on Him when we cry out for help. Our faith speaks out and the Word of God becomes alive and flows out through us.

Prayer Is a Channel

Prayer is the channel through which all good flows from God to man—forgiveness, healing, power, love. Prayer is a way of knowing God. We must also recognize that prayer is a privilege and not to be taken lightly. It becomes our channel of touching God.

While prayer can be uplifting, it can also be a battleground where Satan can attack us. It is in the place of prayer that we engage the devil; but we engage him with the victory already won for us at Calvary. We do warfare with the enemy in the authority of the crucified, risen and ascended Lord and we need not fear the devil and his entrapments.

Prayer is a Progression

The progression of prayer can be compared to the stages and levels of school. You begin at a level where it is very elementary and you continue to learn the more you progress in your spiritual walk. Prayer is simple, yet it is unlimited. A child can voice a simple prayer to God, yet the greatest saint never learns all there is to prayer.

Prayer is a Partnership

The more you pray the more you realize that prayer is a partnership. It is God and man working together, "discussing" problems and counseling together to see the will of God in a given circumstance. As we develop a partnership, it becomes a relationship; a relationship in which we can come boldly to Him at any time, anywhere and for any thing.

God understands all languages. God is everywhere at all times. He welcomes us to come and pray.

COMMUNICATING WITH GOD

Genesis, the first book of the Bible, records the creation of man:

"Then God said, 'Let us make man in our image, according to our likeness; let them have dominion . . . over all the earth' . . . then God blessed them and spoke to them" (Genesis 1:26, 27, 28). God spoke their language and they spoke His.

The last book of the Bible declares:

"Thou are worthy, O Lord, to receive glory and honor and power: for thou has created all things, and for thy pleasure they are and were created" (Revelation 4:11, KJV).

Talk With God

Jehovah God, the I AM God, the Triune Father, Son and Holy Spirit God takes pleasure in you and wants to talk with you. He wants to walk with you—to have fellowship with you.

It started out that way in the Garden of Eden before disobedience and sin separated God and man. We don't know how long the perfect state existed but we do know that one day when God came "walking in the garden in the cool of the day," He found that Adam and Eve "hid from the presence of the Lord God among the trees of the garden" (Genesis 3:8). Why? Because they had sinned and they felt guilt and shame.

Walk With God

But God did not walk away from them. He called, "Where are you?" And He asked them some painful questions: "Who told you that you were naked?" "What is this you have done?" (Genesis 3:11, 13). This begins the never-ending search of God for His creation, and His call for them to return to His love, fellowship, and communication with Him through prayer

God Speaks to Us

God speaks to us in many ways: "The heavens declare the glory of God; the skies proclaim the work of his hands" (Psalm 19:1). He speaks through the Scriptures, the church, the Holy Spirit, ministers, friends, inspiration, dreams, visions, direct revelation and more.

God calls to us . . .

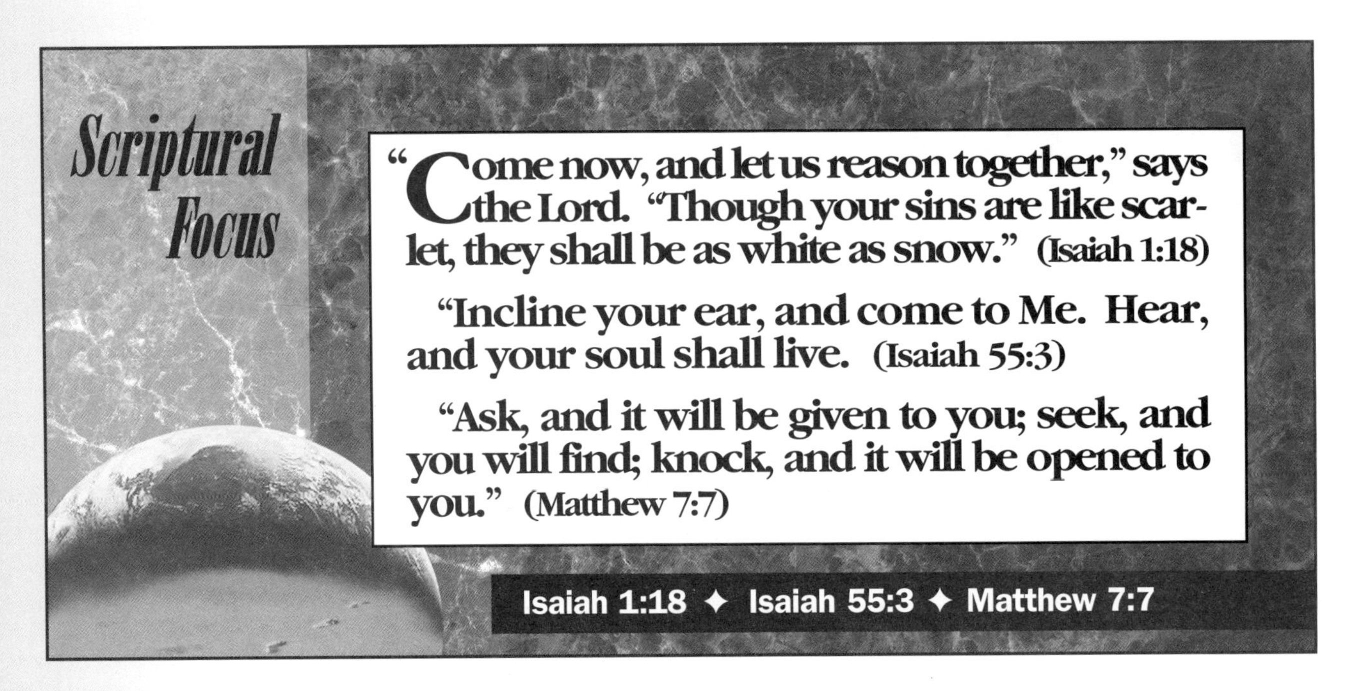

God Provides for You

God wants to have fellowship with you personally and intimately. He communicates to the whole world through His provision of a beautiful earth to live in, through the provision of food, water, air, health and endless other gifts.

God Speaks Through His Word

One of the greatest gifts is His Word—the Holy Bible. He will speak to you through the written word, and even more, He will make the Bible come alive to meet your needs.

But the Lord wants to be directly involved in our lives. He does not force His way. He chooses to give us freedom of choice. He wants us to partner with Him. He waits for our invitation. He sadly tells us, "Behold! I stand at the door and knock" (Revelation 3:20). He says this to His church.

God's Names for His Children

God calls us His sheep, His body, His bride, His church, the apple of His eye, His vineyard, and He waits for us to come to Him, to open the door and invite Him in. We do that when we come to Him in prayer.

Applying the Truth

MY DAILY WALK WITH GOD

Prayer Checklist

As you begin an earnest prayer life, it is important to remember the elements of prayer that have been discussed. Fill in the blanks:

Prayer is ______ God.	Prayer is ______.
Recognizing that He IS	A channel
Acknowledging	Crying out for help
Talking with	The Word of God becoming alive in us
Listening to	Faith speaking out
Praising	Forgiveness
Loving	Healing
Obeying	Love
Waiting on	A privilege
A way of knowing	A worship
Touching	Work
Humbling ourselves in worship to	Warfare

HOW GOD ANSWERS

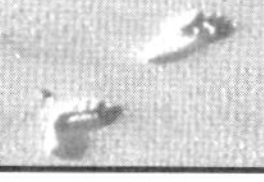

God does answer. You can count on it. You have His own word on it. He says, "Call to me and I will answer you" (Jeremiah 33:3). Daniel proved that statement when he called on God while in exile and God revealed mysteries of the end times. He even sent archangel Gabriel in person to tell Daniel he was loved and to explain the delay in receiving the answer (Daniel 9:10).

God Answers in Many Ways

God answers in more than one way. Sometimes He says *yes*; sometimes He says *no*; sometimes he says *wait*; sometimes He surprises us with unexpected answers. Sometimes it's easy to get impatient. We may not even recognize the answer because it's not the way we wanted or expected it.

Jesus Is the Messiah

Think about this: The Jewish people prayed for the coming of the Messiah. They prophesied of His coming and supposedly looked for the Messiah. But when the Messiah—Jesus—came only a few recognized Him. Most still think God has not yet answered their prayers. Anna and Simeon recognized Him (Luke 2:25-36); the wise men, the Magi, all recognized Him (Matthew 2:1, 2); the woman at the well in Samaria said, "I know that Messiah [called Christ] is coming. When he comes, he will explain everything to us." Then Jesus declared, "I who speak to you am He." But rather than believe this, the Jewish religious leaders plotted His death.

Don't Give Up

Some people give up too soon. The light of faith goes off, the prayer ceases; they give up before the angel can deliver the package. The Bible says, "Elijah was a man just like us. He prayed . . . again he prayed" (James 5:17, 18). Jesus taught the parable of the persistent widow who kept going to the unjust judge asking for justice. Finally he said, "because this widow keeps bothering me, I will see that she gets justice." Then Jesus said, "And will not God bring about justice to his chosen who cry out to him day and night? . . . I tell you he will see that they get justice, and quickly" (Luke 18). Luke 18:1 says, "Jesus told his disciples a [this] parable to show them they should always pray and not give up."

Biblical Examples of Answered Prayer

Biblical examples of prayers God answered:

- Manna (bread) from the sky (Exodus 16:4, 5)
- Water from a rock (Exodus 17:4-6)
- Quail (meat) to eat (Exodus 16:11-13)
- The sun stood still (Joshua 10:12-14)
- The tempest is stilled (Matthew 8:23-27)
- Lazarus is raised from the dead (John 11:38-45)
- Daniel is delivered from lions (Daniel 6:16-23)
- Demons are cast out (Matthew 8:28-32)
- David defeats Goliath (1 Samuel 17:32-51)
- A virgin gives birth to a Savior (Luke 1:30; 2:10-16)
- A crippled woman's spine is straightened (Luke 13:10-13)
- Satan is defeated (Luke 10:18).

Are you crippled, in a storm, fighting demon powers, being persecuted, in need of food, provision? God shows He is able to solve any problem! Ask, believe, trust, hold on, don't give up, give thanks, sing, praise—put everything in the hands of the God who loves you—PRAY.

Applying the Truth

MY DAILY WALK WITH GOD

- True or False ___I really believe that God answers prayer.
- True or False ___I believe the Bible teaches that God answers prayer.
- True or False ___I know God has answered prayers for me.

True or False ___I believe that God gives the best when we leave the choice with Him.

True or False ___I believe God is good, and in His will is my peace.

List prayers God has answered for you.____________________

____

____

What is your most urgent current prayer request?____________

____

____

ASPECTS OF PRAYER

Center of Prayer

The center of prayer is God. We should not focus on our problems, our needs, or even the needs of others. We should focus on God. Loving Him, listening to Him, worshiping Him obeying Him, thanking Him, praising Him should be the heart of prayer. This makes prayer positive and powerful.

Goal of Prayer

God's will is the goal of prayer. Prayer is saying *yes* to God. It is letting Him set our desires. It is getting to know God and understanding His will and purpose in our life.

Prayer Works

Prayer works because God answers. Prayer works because God is alive and He loves every human being. God is a personal, living, loving Father who wants to do wonderful things through us and for us. God is at the other end of prayer.

Prayer is . . .

Prayer is thanksgiving, gratitude, praise and adoration. Prayer is commitment. Prayer is believing God, rejoicing in God. It is contact with divine Presence. It is living communion with God. Through prayer we come into the experience of the living Christ.

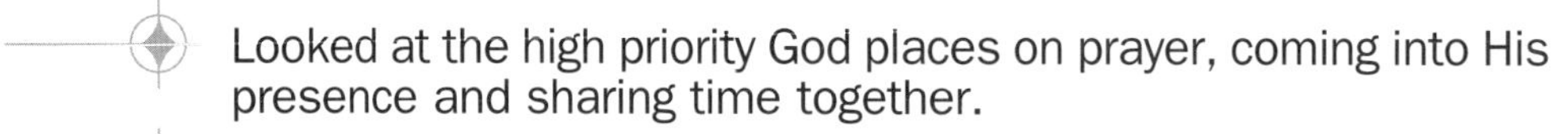

LESSON REVIEW

We have:

- Looked at the high priority God places on prayer, coming into His presence and sharing time together.
- Talked about understanding the many facets of prayer—listening as well as talking, praise, adoring, loving, singing, giving thanks, obeying.
- Discussed the pathway of prayer that leads to the storehouse of the rich resources of God, forgiveness, acceptance, guidance, deliverance, strength, comfort, fellowship, communion, protection, healing, and more.
- Rejoiced in God's welcome and His urging us to come, and His love and eagerness to receive us.
- Considered Biblical models, examples, challenges, and demonstrations of glorious victories for those who do come.

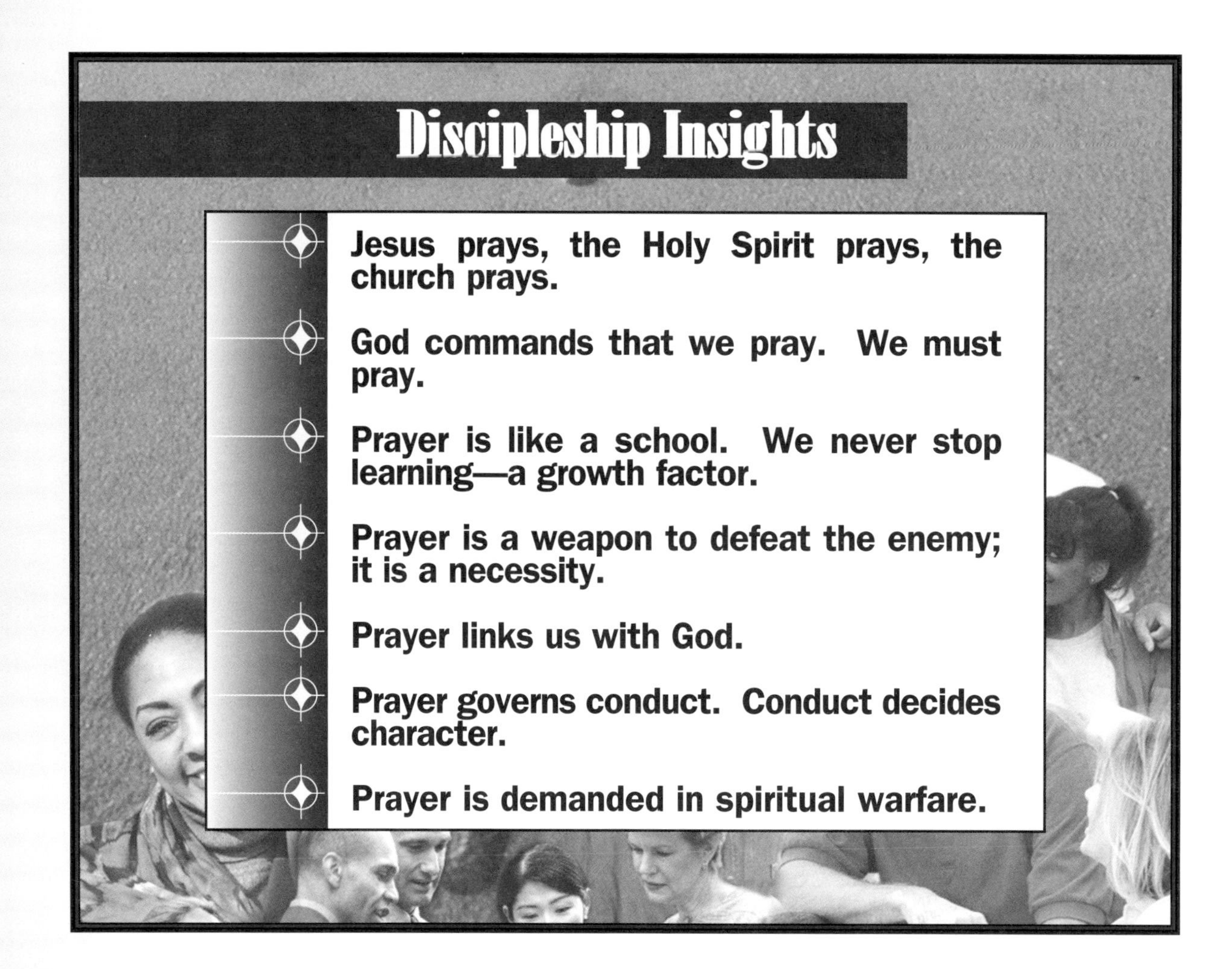

Discipleship Insights

- **Jesus prays, the Holy Spirit prays, the church prays.**
- **God commands that we pray. We must pray.**
- **Prayer is like a school. We never stop learning—a growth factor.**
- **Prayer is a weapon to defeat the enemy; it is a necessity.**
- **Prayer links us with God.**
- **Prayer governs conduct. Conduct decides character.**
- **Prayer is demanded in spiritual warfare.**

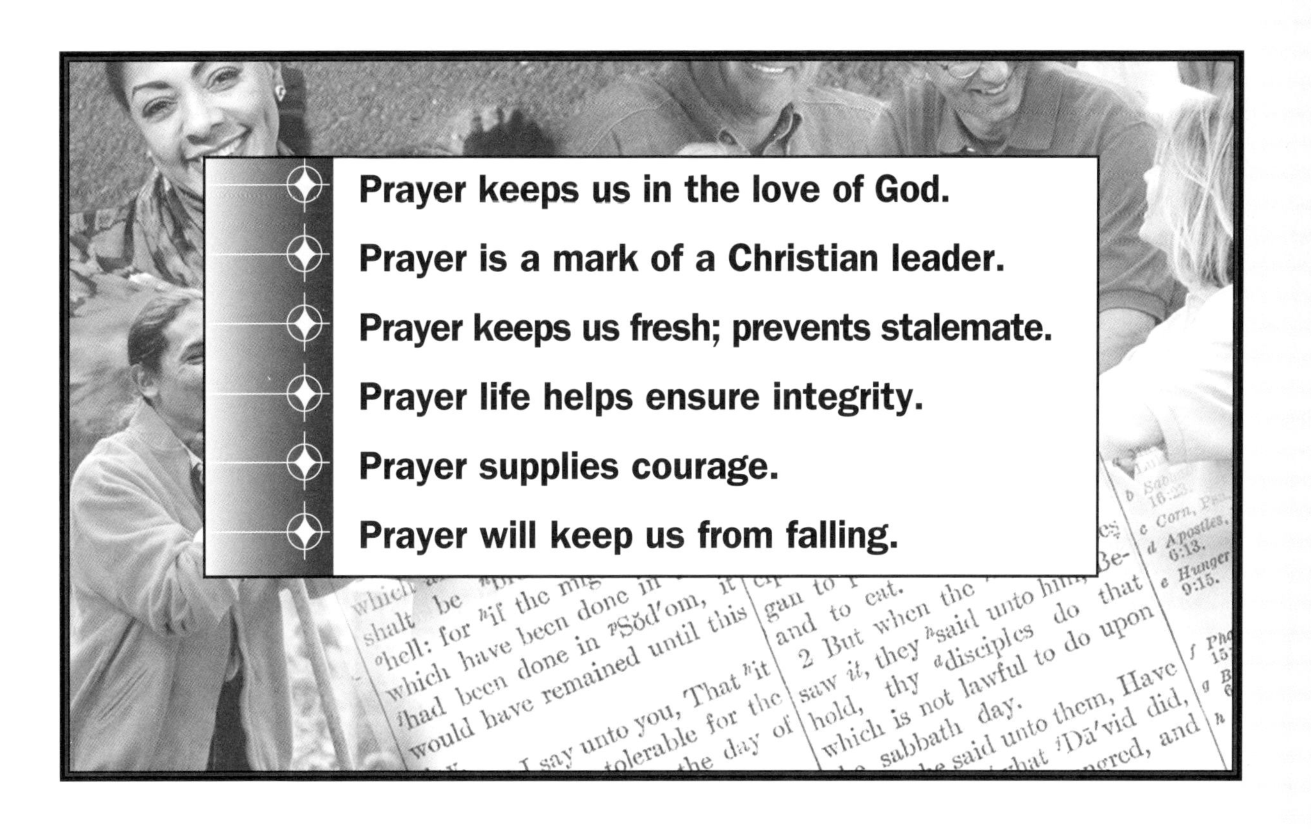
Prayer keeps us in the love of God.
Prayer is a mark of a Christian leader.
Prayer keeps us fresh; prevents stalemate.
Prayer life helps ensure integrity.
Prayer supplies courage.
Prayer will keep us from falling.

NOTES: ____________________

WORSHIP

The Believer's Highest Privilege

5
LESSON

John D. Childers

INTRODUCTION

Highest Privilege

Worship is the highest privilege we have as Christians. Therefore, it should be the primary focus of believers, both individually and in the congregational setting. When we worship the Father we reestablish the Biblical chain of command and join with all creation in recognizing the King of Kings and Lord of Lords.

In worship we ascribe worth to someone or something. Biblical worship is accomplished by recognizing that God is Creator, Redeemer, and Sustainer. Through the awesome abilities of God, the universe continues to exist. Through our worship of the Creator we celebrate life at its fullest level because we have an intimate relationship with God through His Son, the Chief Cornerstone.

Worship Is Where God Lives

Worship is where God lives. He inhabits the praises of His people. He is enthroned and liberated to act mightily in praise. The church is likened to a spiritual building, a temple for the habitation of God through the Spirit:

> Now, therefore, you are no longer strangers and foreigners, but fellow citizens with the saints and members of the household of God, having been built on the foundation of the apostles and prophets, Jesus Christ himself being the chief cornerstone, in whom the whole building, being joined together, grows into a holy temple in the Lord, in whom you also are being built together for a dwelling place of God in the Spirit (Ephesians 2:19-22).

Worship Is Ministry to the Lord

Worship is ministry to the Lord. Just as there was a gate into the tabernacle, there is a gateway into the worship experience:

> Make a joyful shout to the LORD, all you lands! Serve the LORD with gladness; Come before His presence with singing. Know

that the LORD, He is God; It is He who has made us, and not we ourselves; We are His people and the sheep of His pasture. Enter into His gates with thanksgiving, And into His courts with praise. Be thankful to Him, and bless His name. For the LORD is good; His mercy is everlasting, And His truth endures to all generations (Psalm 100:1-5, *NKJV*).

Worship is not only praise and adoration to God for who He is, but it is also knowing who we are in Him and sharing that news with others in ministry.

Worship is a garment of praise that enables us to ward off the spirit of heaviness (depression). It is a power tool to use against the enemy.

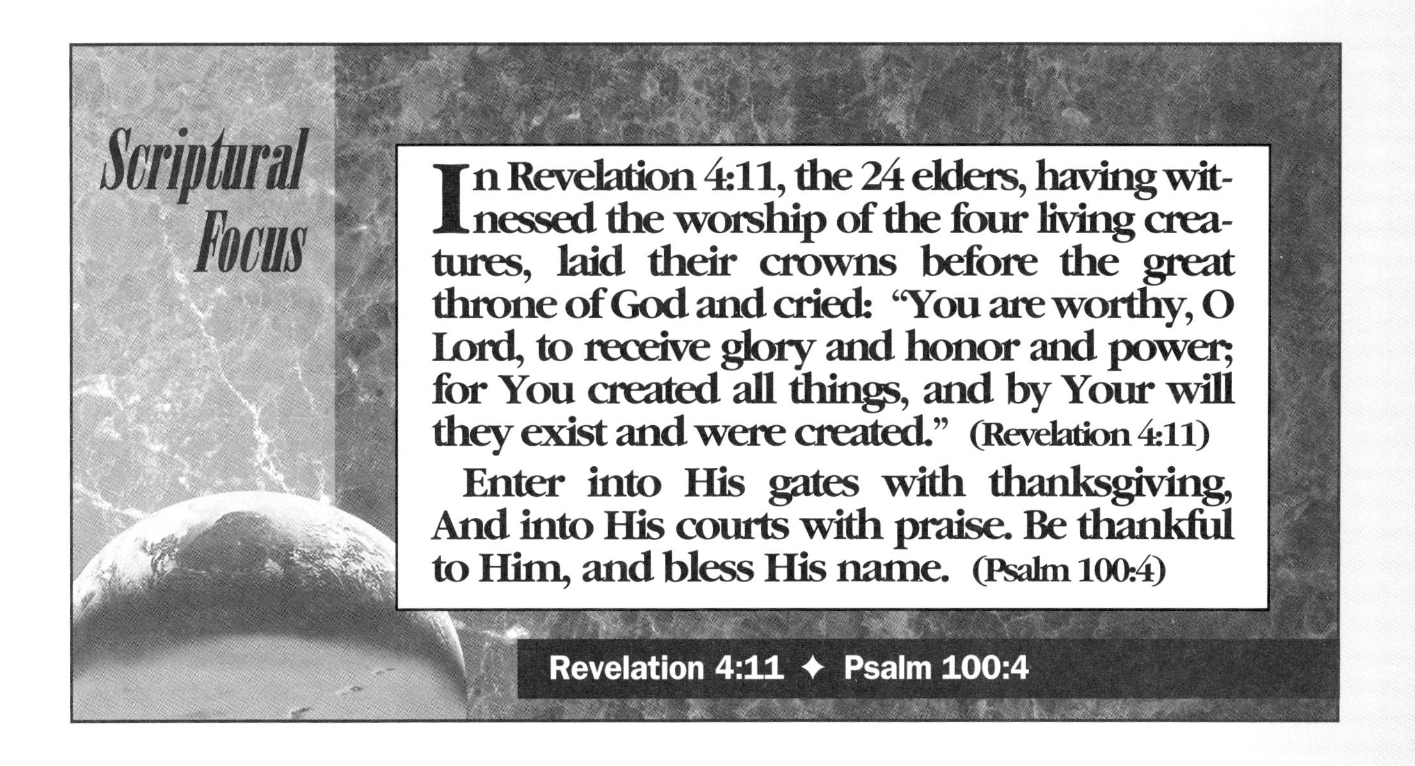

THE ESSENCE OF WORSHIP

A Response to God

The word *worship* is used by many Christians for a wide variety of experiences and impressions. Worship should speak principally about one's response to God. Worship is an active response to God whereby we declare His worth. Worship is not passive, but is participative. It is not simply a mood; it is a response. It is not just a feeling; it is a declaration.

Declare His Worth

The English word comes from the Anglo-Saxon "weorthscipe," which then was modified to "worthship," and finally to "worship." To worship someone or something is to attribute supreme worth or to declare supreme value to that one or that thing. To worship God is to ascribe to Him supreme worth, for He alone is worthy.

He Is Worthy

Because of who God is and what He does, we attribute to Him the glory that is due His name. Psalms 96:4, 6-9 says, "For the Lord is great and greatly to be praised; He is to be feared above all gods. Honor and majesty are before Him; strength and beauty are in His sanctuary. Give to the Lord, O families of the peoples, give to the Lord glory and strength. Give to the Lord the glory due His name; bring an offering, and come into His courts. Oh, worship the Lord in the beauty of holiness!"

Celebrate Him

The essence of worship is the celebration of God! When we worship God, we celebrate Him; we extol Him, we sound His praises, we boast in Him.

Worship is communication and relationship with God. In his book, *The Ministry of Church and Pastor*, Paul L. Walker says:

Worship Is Relationship With God

> However, to communicate and have relationship with God, it is important for us to see the factors which bring this definition of worship into focus:
>
> 1. *Worship is thanksgiving:* It is to give thanks in glad response to the holy, redemptive love of God made known in Jesus Christ.
> 2. *Worship is offering:* It is to offer one's self to God in common worship with others who make up the body of Christ as we, who are many, are one body in Christ.
> 3. *Worship is edification:* It is to edify God in the cultivation of discipleship, prayer, and forgiveness.
> 4. *Worship is service:* It is to become a living sacrifice engaged in the Christian life in the world.
> 5. *Worship is response:* In a word, worship is the response of the body of Christians to the revelation of God in Jesus Christ (p. 50).

WORSHIP IS WHERE GOD LIVES

The Psalmist recognized that God lives in the praises of His people when he wrote, "But You are holy, enthroned in the praises of Israel" (22:3).

God Lives in the Praises of His People

Since the time of Adam and Eve's sin and subsequent fall in the Garden of Eden, God has been in the process of restoring mankind to a proper relationship with Himself. The path of renewing God's people can be traced through the pages of His Word.

In his book, *Ministry and Theology*, John Christopher Thomas describes the process this way: "The Old Testament believers looked forward to the Messiah and were justified in advance, while the New Testament believers are able to look back on what has been accomplished. Abraham is the example of how God deals with human beings. Because he believed, Abraham was counted righteous" (p. 22).

After Noah, the Bible pictures God as living afar off. He would come down to see what man was up to (Genesis 11:5). Whenever God confronted man face to face, man was frightened. This was Jacob's experience when he awoke from an encounter with God: "Then Jacob awoke from his sleep and said, 'Surely the Lord is in this place, and I did not know it.' And he was afraid and said, 'How awesome is this place! This is none other than the house of God, and this is the gate of heaven!'" (Genesis 28:16, 17).

But then God came closer when He called Moses to Sinai. Though the Ten Commandments took center stage in this encounter, the other message from the mountain was just as incredible: "God is coming to guide us personally!"

God laid out the specifications for the construction of a beautiful tent. The Lord of heaven and earth desired a physical home for His people.

The tent tabernacle became not only the center of Jewish worship, but also the source of guidance for Israel. In Habakkuk's day, the portable tabernacle was replaced with the stationary temple—a place to inquire of the Lord and seek His will. But God wanted to move His guidance system closer to man. Through the miracle of the Virgin Birth, the Creator offered humanity the kind of relationship not known since the Garden of Eden. God put on flesh. He walked the dusty streets of Palestine in the body of Jesus of Nazareth. Mankind could actually walk and talk with God. No closer relationship could have been imagined, but God came nearer still.

The Holy Spirit Guides Us

When Jesus left His followers on earth, He promised that the Holy Spirit would be given: "Behold, I send the Promise of My Father upon you; but tarry in the city of Jerusalem until you are endued with power from on high" (Luke 24:49). Through the powerful presence of the Holy Spirit, God provides personal guidance, personal comfort, and personal worship to His people.

Applying the Truth

MY DAILY WALK WITH GOD

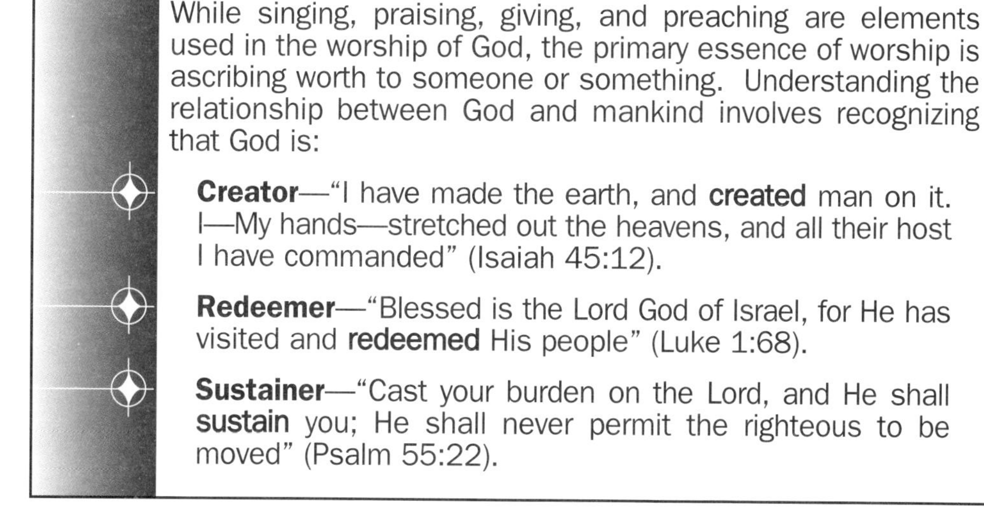

While singing, praising, giving, and preaching are elements used in the worship of God, the primary essence of worship is ascribing worth to someone or something. Understanding the relationship between God and mankind involves recognizing that God is:

Creator—"I have made the earth, and **created** man on it. I—My hands—stretched out the heavens, and all their host I have commanded" (Isaiah 45:12).

Redeemer—"Blessed is the Lord God of Israel, for He has visited and **redeemed** His people" (Luke 1:68).

Sustainer—"Cast your burden on the Lord, and He shall **sustain** you; He shall never permit the righteous to be moved" (Psalm 55:22).

WORSHIP IS MINISTRY TO THE LORD

In Acts 2, we find a description of early Christian worship: "And they continued steadfastly in the apostles' doctrine and fellowship, in the breaking of bread, and in prayers" (v. 42). "So continuing daily with one accord in the temple, and breaking bread from house to house, they ate their food with gladness and simplicity of heart, praising God and having favor with all the people. And the Lord added to the church daily those who were being saved" (vv. 46, 47).

Origins of Church Worship

In his book, *The Ministry of Church and Pastor*, Paul L. Walker says:

> The origins of Christian worship lie in the first communion between God and man and were expressed in the altar and the tabernacle. Out of this heritage of the tent, carried with the wandering Hebrews, developed the temple in Palestine and the synagogue in every community of the covenant people. Apostolic worship celebrated the coming of the Messiah and His resurrection through praise, prayer, scripture, and sacrament. Even during the most severe persecutions by the Roman authorities in the first three centuries of the Roman era worship continued in the catacombs and secret places. Out of this development one fact has clearly emerged throughout succeeding centuries—worship is essentially social; it goes out to God and it fosters the highest fellowship of spirit between man and man" (pp. 50, 51).

Spiritual Gifts

Through the Holy Spirit, believers are graciously furnished with the gifts necessary to fulfill the mission and ministry of the church. A list of spiritual gifts reveals the Holy Spirit has varied the gifts in order to serve the total needs of the church. Spiritual gifts involve preaching, giving, teaching, administration, helping, and many more (1 Corinthians 12:1-12; Romans 12:6-8; Ephesians 4:11). The purpose of these gifts is that the whole body of the church may be equipped for service (1 Corinthians 12:7).

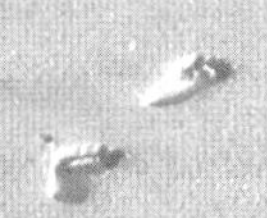

WORSHIP IS A GARMENT THAT WARDS OFF THE SPIRIT OF HEAVINESS

Worship Is a Garment of Praise

Despite all the advancements in the medical world, nothing wards off the heaviness of discouragement and doubt as well as true worship. Depression and praise cannot coexist in the heart. This truth is perhaps nowhere more eloquently expressed than in Isaiah 61:1-3:

> "The Spirit of the Lord God is upon Me,
>
> Because the Lord has anointed Me
>
> To preach good tidings to the poor;
>
> He has sent Me to heal the brokenhearted,

To proclaim liberty to the captives,
And the opening of the prison to those who are bound;
To proclaim the acceptable year of the Lord,
And the day of vengeance of our God;
To comfort all who mourn,
To console those who mourn in Zion,
To give them beauty for ashes,
The oil of joy for mourning,
The garment of praise for the spirit of heaviness;
That they may be called trees of righteousness,
The planting of the Lord, that He may be glorified."

Nothing terrifies the devil and his demons like worship from the depths of a believer's heart. In worship we enter the presence of God where the powers of darkness are not welcome. One minister described this type of praise as putting on a topcoat. It is that easy.

Applying the Truth

MY DAILY WALK WITH GOD

When we make the choice to put on the garment of praise daily, then we reap the benefits of this choice . . .

- In His presence . . . there is healing.
- In His presence . . . there is freedom.
- In His presence . . . there is celebration.
- In His presence . . . there is ransom from sin.
- In His presence . . . there is hope.
- In His presence . . . there is love.
- In His presence . . . there is power.
- In His presence . . . there is deliverance.

WORSHIP—THE POWER TOOL AGAINST THE ENEMY

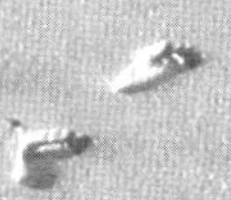

Christ commanded His disciples to wait in Jerusalem until they were endued with power from on high. The Holy Spirit is the source of power against the enemy.

PRAISE WILL STAND IN YOUR DAILY BATTLES

Worship Is a Spiritual Weapon

In the Old Testament Jehosophat was informed that a coalition of enemy armies was advancing toward the palace in such numbers that there was no possibility of surviving the attack. He turned to the Lord whose face he sought daily. God's answer came quickly through the prophet: "Do not be afraid nor dismayed because of this great multitude, for the battle is not yours, but God's" (2 Chronicles 20:15). They faced the enemy with the sole weapon of worship—a one-line chorus singing, "Give thanks to the Lord, for His love endures forever" (21, 22).

The Hebrew word *yadah* means "to give thanks with hands extended." The army of Jehosophat went into battle expecting to do warfare against the enemy. However, they found to their great surprise the giant coalition of armies dead on the field. Worship prepared the way and implemented their deliverance.

WORSHIP REVEALS THE WILL OF GOD FOR OUR LIVES

Worship Reveals God's Will

Jonah disobeyed God's instructions to preach to the city of Nineveh. He fled from the presence of God and complicated not only his problem, but endangered the others on board the ship. However, when Jonah began to worship he sang, "But I, with a song of thanksgiving, will sacrifice to you. What I have vowed I will make good. Salvation comes from the LORD" (Jonah 2:9, NIV). At this point Jonah found deliverance. God commanded the fish to unload its passenger onto dry land.

WORSHIP BREAKS THE BONDAGE

Worship Neutralizes Evil Influence

Paul and Silas were imprisoned in a cold, dark Philippian jail. But at midnight while they were praying and singing hymns to God, a violent earthquake shook the foundation of the prison, breaking the hinges off the doors and freeing the prisoners from their shackles. Before day broke, the jailer and his family were prisoners of Jesus Christ. The magistrates released Paul and Silas who departed the city in peace (Acts 16:25-40).

Why is it that demons are devastated by our worship to the Lord? Could it be that Satan, in his original state as Lucifer, might have been the praise and worship leader in heaven? In his desire to be greater than God, Lucifer took a risk and lost. Since then he and his demons inflict misery on human beings and try to stop their praise. But when they encounter Biblical worship, they are driven back. Their influence is neutralized and their evil exposed by worship.

LESSON REVIEW

It is easy to confuse an emotional reaction to certain stimuli with an act of worship. When we worship, we join with all creation in recognizing the Chief Cornerstone. By worshipping God we are enabled by the Holy Spirit to ward off the spirit of heaviness of the enemy, and to minister to others. But worship is every individual's choice. No one can force us to worship. Worship erupts from a heart of gratitude and praise.

Worship has international proportions. It influences nations, kings, princes, and people. The mandate to praise and worship is not unusual. What is unusual and astounding is the manifold purposes of combining praises with the Word of truth. "For the Lord takes delight in His people. He crowns the humble with salvation. Let the saints rejoice in this honor (worship) and sing for joy on their beds. May the praise of God be in their mouths and a double-edge sword in their hands . . . to inflict vengeance on the nations and punishment on the people, to bind their kings with fetters, their nobles with shackles of iron, to carry out the sentence written against them. This is the glory of all his saints. Praise the Lord" (Psalm 149:4-9).

Everyone who worships God in spirit and in truth He invites to:

- Enjoy every benefit of forgiveness
- Receive every provision of victory
- Enter into freedom from every bondage
- Partake of His healing presence and power
- What more could we ask?

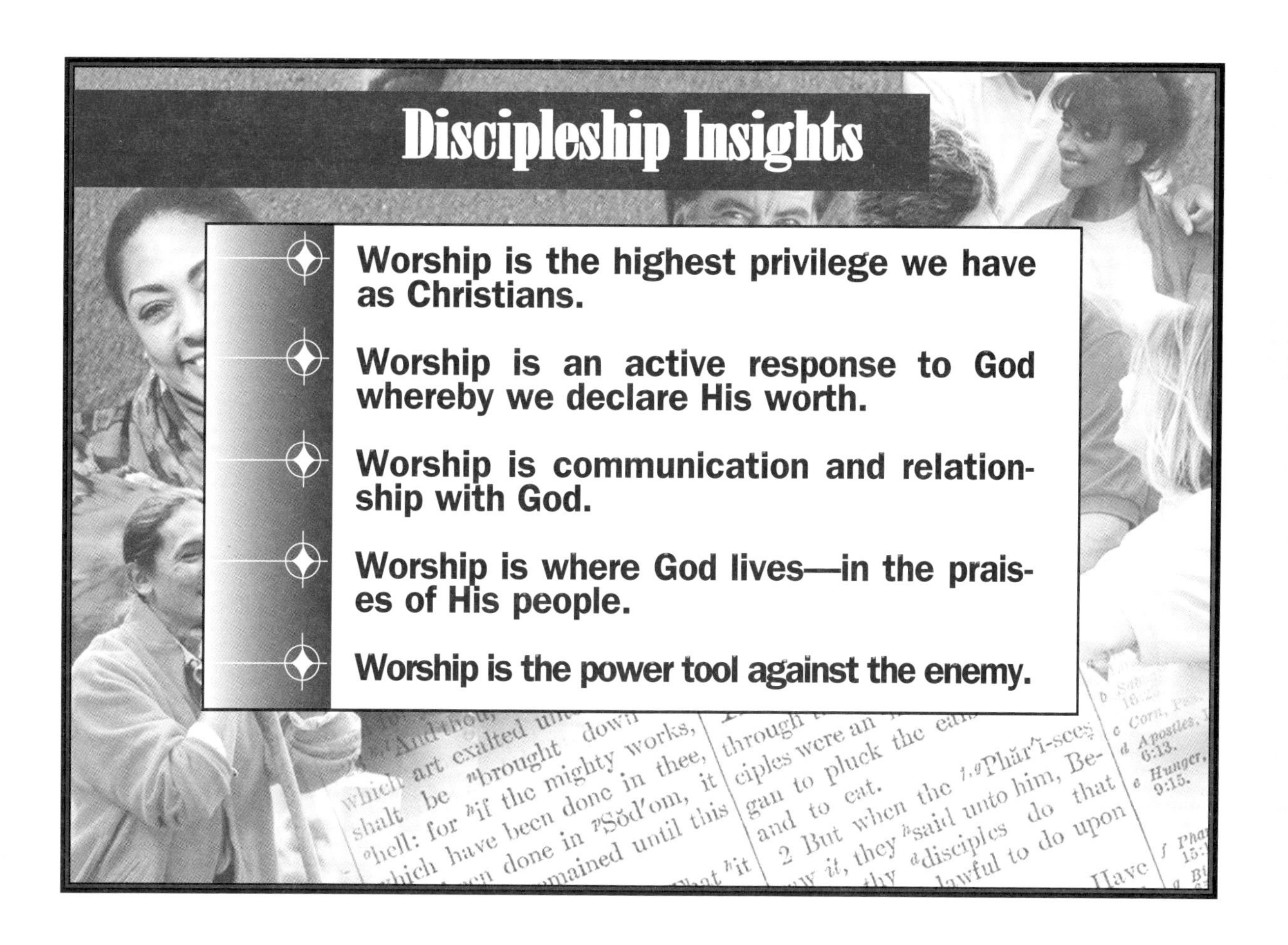

RESOURCES

Hayford, Jack W., *Worship His Majesty*. Waco, Texas: Word Books, 1987.

Sims, John A., *Our Pentecostal Heritage*. Cleveland, Tenn.: Pathway Press, 1995.

Thomas, John Christopher, *Ministry and Theology*. Cleveland, Tenn.: Pathway Press, 1996.

Walling, Jeff, *Daring to Dance with God*. West Monroe, Louisiana: Howard Publishing Co., 1996.

Walker, Paul L., *The Ministry of Church and Pastor*. Cleveland, Tenn.: Pathway Press, 1965.

NOTES:

STEWARDSHIP

Supervising God's Provisions

Al Taylor

INTRODUCTION

Scripture has much to say about our role as *stewards* in God's service. The Biblical record will show that God intended for each of us to be a resource manager from the beginning. The consequences of that assignment are great. Our individual spiritual condition is revealed constantly in the realm of possessions. The authority of this divine assignment, the opportunity for faithful performance, and the certainty of rewards constitute the "good news" about an integral part of our Christian experience.

God has invited us into His family and into the family business. Let's examine what He has to say about (1) our resources; (2) our responsibilities; (3) our rewards; and (4) our relationships.

Scriptural Focus

Then God said, "Let Us make man in Our likeness, according to Our likeness; let them have dominion over the fish of the sea, over the birds of the air, and over the cattle, over all the earth and over every creeping thing that creeps on the earth."

Genesis 1:26

RESOURCES

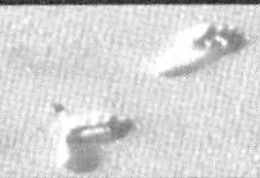

Created Man

When God created man He placed him in a world of resources. Man was made from the dust of the earth and given dominion over the creation around him. God breathed into the nostrils of His created man, and man became a living soul. Because man is spirit, he is capable of fellowship and communion with God. Because man is soul, he has intellect—a free will and the intelligence to exercise it. Because man is body, he has authority in the physical realm. He can move things around.

Man's Choice

God allowed man to exercise his physical, mental, and spiritual abilities in the Garden of Eden. He was protected there; and, although everything was good in Eden, God also provided "choice." It would be meaningless for man to be created with the capacity for free will and then have no meaningful decisions to make. The very act of making decisions builds character and molds personality.

Man's Dominion

Man's "assigned dominion" did not replace God's "ultimate dominion." Man had rulership, but he was an underruler. He had decision-making ability and authority, but he did not have "God prerogative." For example, man can make good decisions or bad decisions. The good decisions lead to good results and bad decisions lead to bad results. But man cannot control those consequences. God sets the consequences and only He has the power to interrupt, change, or delay them. Men are prone to waste a good portion of their lives and resources in the futility of trying to deny, change, or avoid the consequences of their bad decisions and bad actions.

Stewardship

To better understand the divine assignment of dominion, we commonly refer to it as "stewardship" or "trusteeship." "Steward" is more often used as a word depicting career or profession. Trustee is indeed a key part of the steward's role but may be only a minor part of one's responsibilities. Steward is a person entrusted with valuable assets which he is to manage for the owner according to the owner's instructions and with the understanding of accountability to the owner.

Entrustment

God has entrusted to each individual a trust of time, a trust of possessions, a trust of abilities, and a trust of communication. Obviously, we are not given matching amounts of anything but the rule is the same for each: follow the owner's instructions. A significant potential exists for each of us to increase our capacity to be entrusted with more. We rise to new levels of stewardship through obedience.

God is owner of all creation because He is the Creator. In a very real sense the Bible is a deed. It describes property, it identifies the owner, and it tells how He obtained the property. As the owner God has the right to do whatever He chooses to do with it. He has chosen to entrust it to us in varying proportions.

There are limits placed by the owner, chief of which is time itself. We will all release the property in our trust at a time defined by the owner.

Disobedience

When the first couple God created was tempted to disobey the owner's instructions regarding the property entrusted to them, they chose disobedience. The spiritual temptation was "you can be as gods." The expression of that temptation was physical. They ate that which the owner said "don't eat." Pride had betrayed them. Their effort to overrule the owner—the true God—reduced them to a state of "fallenness." They had been offered "image of God" in their lives through a relationship of communion with God. They were offered "likeness of God" through learning and obedience. Instead, they tried Satan's shortcut: a false promise that you can be as God by defiance of His instructions.

Man fell by choosing to believe something other than what God said. Then he expressed that unbelief by acting it out in disobedience through his stewardship—he consumed what the owner forbade. The created material was not bad. God had already declared it good. The evil was not in the things man had been given. They only provided the opportunity to express the evil in man's heart. The evil in his heart did not reside there until he chose to act contrary to God's Word.

Before the fall Adam and Eve had never known insecurity. God was their source. They walked with Him daily. They had all their needs met in Him. After the fall they sought security in things. That pursuit led to the love of things and to idolatry. Man's problems were becoming worse because of a very bad decision to go in the wrong direction.

Jesus taught us, "whoever of you does not forsake all that he has cannot be my disciple" (Luke 14:33). That is the good news regarding resources. Each of us comes to God from a position of sin or fallenness. In the sinful condition possessions are terribly important to us. In a certain respect we all come to Christ from idolatry. Until we repent of our sins and submit to His lordship, we are in the grip of possessions.

God's Call to Stewardship

Idolatry is that condition wherein any part of creation is so important to us that we place it between us and the Creator in our affections. Jesus makes clear in this verse that we are not only to return to Him for salvation, but we are also to deliberately and willfully place every possession under His ownership. The title *Lord* means owner as in landlord. When we forsake our ownership of things we then enjoy the calling to be God's steward. We are then free to use things as the true owner directs, which releases blessing to us and makes us a blessing.

The story is often told of how easy it is to trap a monkey. The trap is designed with an opening just large enough for the monkey's open hand to reach through. When the monkey's hand grasps the desired trinket or piece of food and closes into a fist, it can no longer be pulled through the opening.

Although the monkey could easily go free if he would release the prize, his nature is such that he will not turn loose. How much are we like the monkey? Or, is the monkey like us?

RESPONSIBILITIES

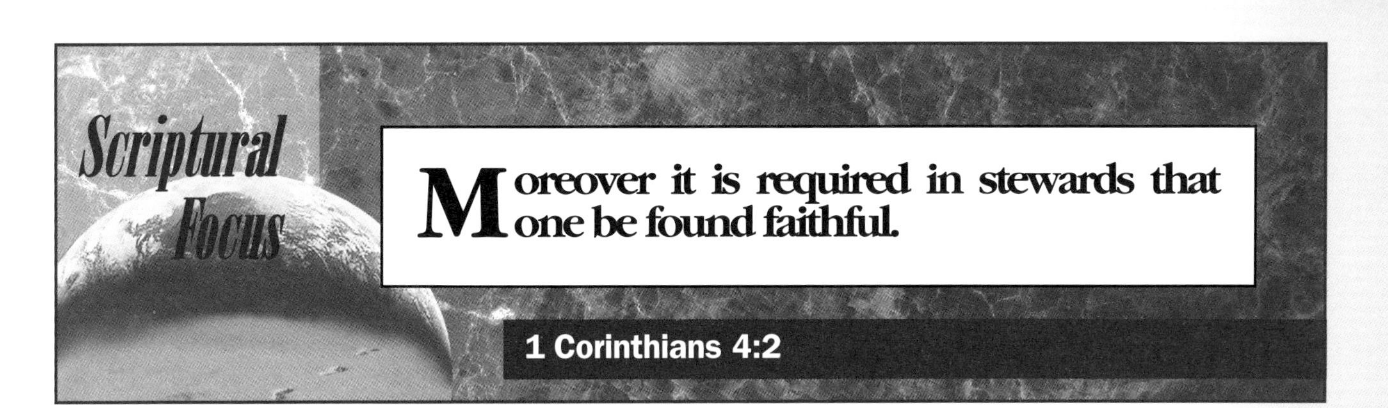

Co-responsibility

One synonym for Biblical stewardship is co-responsibility. God is very serious about the purpose He has set for Himself regarding us. Although there is phenomenal difference in His attributes and our abilities, He has chosen to give us a kind of partnership with Him. He doesn't need our abilities—He has all ability. He doesn't need the resources in our trust—He owns all the universe. Yet, we have a need to grow and develop through fellowship with Him. He includes us in what He is doing as a father teaching His children. Through obedience in the realm of stewardship we are partners with Him in the good things He is doing. We grow by the participation, and we constantly see how good and how real our Father is as our obedience produces blessings for us and others. Thus, the more we grow, the more we know of Him. The more we know Him, the more we desire to be like Him. Through obedience comes blessing and ever-increasing motivation for us to see fulfilled in our life what God originally purposed in our relationship.

Every Disciple Is Called to Be a Steward

The most concise statement of our responsibility is found in Paul's letter to the Corinthians, "Moreover it is required in stewards that one be found faithful" (1 Corinthians 4:2). Each person is called to be a disciple of Christ. Every disciple is to be a steward. As we have already seen (Luke 14:33), we cannot be a disciple of Christ unless we obey the call to be His steward. Stewardship includes every resource under our control. The responsibility of stewardship is expressed in one word, faithful.

Faithful

To be faithful simply means that we follow the Lord's instructions regarding every resource entrusted to us. We are to use every resource the way the owner wants it used.

Study the following chart:

Resource	Response
Time	God is the holder of first place in our time as evidenced by our devotion, worship, family, and work.
Talent	Our abilities are first dedicated to Him in worship and service but will only be used in God-approved ways at all times.
Treasure	We honor the Lord with our substance and with the firstfruits (tithe) of our increase (Proverbs 3:9).
Testimony	Our ability to communicate will always exalt Christ and speak the truth in love (Ephesians 4:15).

Commitments

As these stewardship commitments are lived out, we are committed to live in a way that is consistent with God's call upon our lives to be faithful stewards. We want our lives to be an example and an illustration of faith in Christ and in His Word.

Just as Adam and Eve failed in their stewardship, we recognize the same failure all around us today. Just as Cain's sin regarding the stewardship of his harvest resulted in God's refusal to accept his offering, we see the same Cain-error today as people refuse to obey God's requirement to put Him first as He defines it.

Families are broken and bewildered because of parents' unwillingness to put God first. Nations are weakened and destroyed because God's people fail to speak the truth in love.

Applying the Truth

MY DAILY WALK WITH GOD

Pray this Prayer.

Dear Father, in the name of Jesus I ask You to forgive me for every disobedience in Your call for me to be Your steward. I acknowledge this disobedience as sin. I ask You to break the power of idolatry in my life. I do not desire to be in bondage to things. My desire is to be under the lordship of Jesus. I acknowledge Him as owner of all. I will put Him first in every resource. I will give You the tithe of every increase, Lord Jesus, then I will give and manage all that remains according to Your Word and the Holy Spirit. In Jesus' name. Amen.

REWARDS

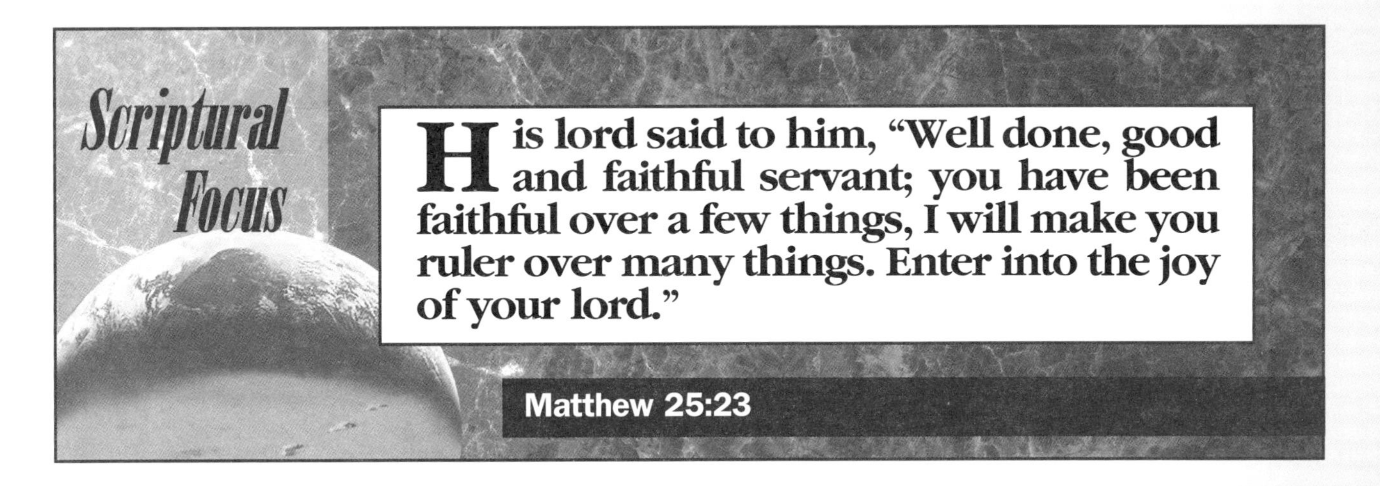

Redemptive Lift

God delights in rewarding faithfulness. The Bible is filled with stories which reveal this great truth about God. The church is also filled with testimonies of God's faithfulness to bless those who obey Him. Historians had to coin a phrase, *redemptive lift*, to describe how consistently God blesses and raises to a new level those who obey Him.

Abraham's Faithfulness

A true story that beautifully reveals this pertinent truth comes from the life of Abraham. In Genesis 13 Abraham and Lot came to a parting of the ways because of their great wealth and the resulting contention among their employees. Abraham unselfishly gave first choice of the land to Lot. Later Lot was taken hostage when four armies defeated all the armies of the Jordan valley and departed with their hostages and all of the transportable wealth of the entire valley (Genesis 14).

Abraham armed his servants, pursued and defeated the armies, rescued Lot, and recovered all of the wealth the armies had confiscated. Upon returning from this unprecedented victory, Abraham first worshiped God, then gave a tithe of all the recovered wealth to Melchizedek (a type of Christ). The King of Sodom announced that the recovered wealth belonged to Abraham (to the victor go the spoils), but Abraham would not accept it. After having tithed the spoils, Abraham gave the 90 percent remaining back to its former owners. And he explained why he did it: "lest you should say, 'I have made Abram rich'" (Genesis 14:23).

The reputation of God was important to Abraham. He wanted everyone to know God was his source. Therefore, he refused a fortune rightfully his to protect the reputation of God.

God responds to this beautiful attitude of Abraham: "After these things the word of the Lord came to Abram in a vision, saying, 'Do not be afraid, Abram. I am your shield, your exceedingly great reward'" (Genesis 15:1).

Abraham had no reason to suffer the insecurity of trusting in things because his trust was in God. God said, "fear not." Abraham had accomplished the impossible: he slaughtered four mighty armies with only 318 servants. God said, "I am your shield." But then came the greatest of all gifts. God said, "I am your exceeding great reward." God announced that because of Abraham's faith and faithfulness he would be rewarded with the ultimate gift: God gave Himself to Abraham.

Our Faithfulness

This same great God of love created you so He could give Himself to you. He only awaits your faith and faithfulness to reveal that you can be trusted with the ultimate gift.

The commands of God carry blessings with them. He loves to bless, but unless we are faithful to His Word the blessings will destroy us. The prosperity of a fool is destruction (Proverbs 1:32). "The fool has said in his heart there is no God" (Psalm 14:1). When my heart denies God and His truth, my prosperity will contribute to my certain failure.

Our Rewards

The rewards of faithfulness in this life only foretell the great day of rewards when we are in full communion with God for all eternity. When we hear Him say, "Well done, good and faithful servant; you were faithful over a few things, I will make you ruler over many things. Enter into the joy of your lord" (Matthew 25:21). That will be worth every sacrifice ever made. To hear those words from our Lord will be the greatest of all rewards.

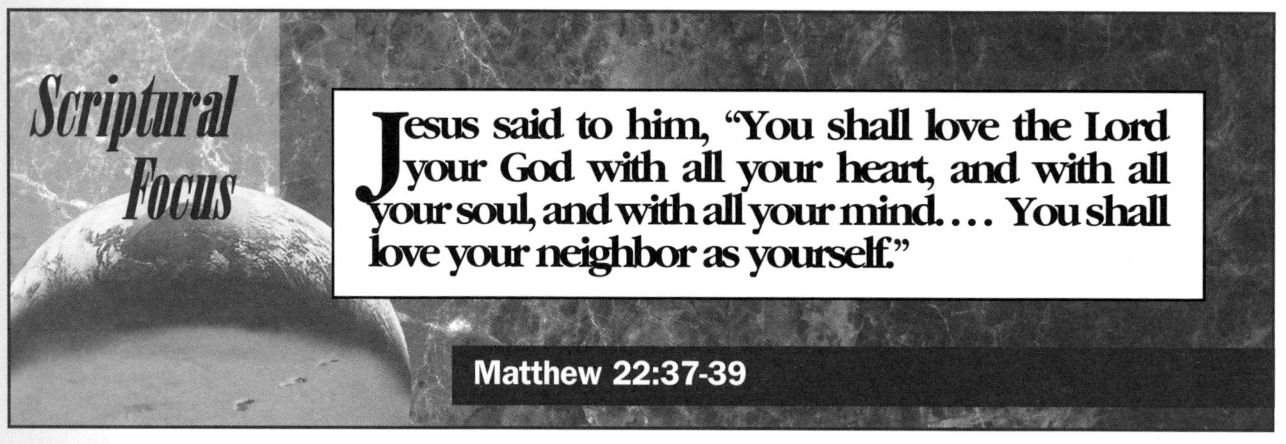

RELATIONSHIPS

Man's love for things and for the money which represents things brings a cruel distortion into life. First, the love of money separates us from God, then it separates us from family. All meaningful relationships are hindered by the love of creation instead of loving the Creator. Here is a chart which shows the Great Commandment with the commandment regarding things added to it.

Great Commandment Chart

The Great Commandment

Truth	Manifest	Product
God is Love Matthew 22:37	Creation	Family
God Loves Mankind John 3:16	Redemption	Presence
Man Loves God John 14:15	Worship	Obedience
Man Loves Man Genesis 12:1, 2	Blessing	Evangelism
Man Loves Self Romans 8:29; 12:1, 2; Matthew 6:33	Submission	Alignment
Man or Mammon 1 Timothy 6:10; 1 John 2:15	Love Not	Stewardship

Satan's Scheme

"You can be like God . . . " Genesis 3:5.

The New Testament Strategy

John 15:7: "If you abide in Me and My words abide in you . . ."

Colossians 2:3: "In whom are hidden all the treasures of wisdom and knowledge."

John 5:39: "You search the scriptures ... and these are they which testify of Me."

Colossians 1:27: "Christ in you, the hope of glory."

Church of God Stewardship Ministries, Cleveland, Tennessee, 1997

Our Relationship to God

As we obey the command to love God, our Creator, we are fulfilled by His presence in our lives. Our lives have meaning and significance because they are properly related to Him. He is glorified by this love relationship because He created us in order to love us and to give Himself to us. His love in our lives enables us to love others, to reveal God's presence in us to the one we are blessing. He enables us to love ourselves in the perspective of truth whereby we can discipline and restrain ourselves.

Love of Things

Then He commands us not to love things. "Do not love the world or the things in the world" (1 John 2:15). If we love things we will use God to try to get more of the creation for our selfish purposes. We will cheat our fellowman to get his stuff. This is the reason why the world denies God and cheats each other—they love stuff—they are idolaters.

On the other hand, if we truly love God then we are free and able to use creation as He directs. We are free to be His steward, to glorify God and to bless everyone whose life we touch.

Applying the Truth

MY DAILY WALK WITH GOD

Let us pray.

Thank you, God, for calling me to be Your steward. I love You, therefore, I am free to obey You and to use any part of creation for Your glory. I put You first in every increase by worshiping You with the tithe. You are Lord. You own me and every resource entrusted to me. Use me for Your glory I pray in Christ's name. Amen.

LESSON REVIEW

We began this study with an emphasis upon resources over which God has given each of us dominion. These are things which we control, at least to some extent, and things on which our choices and decisions have definite impact. On a separate sheet of paper, list your personal resources.

____

____

Since such resources have been placed under our dominion, it follows that we have responsibilities to the One who gave them to us. Review the scriptural focus, 1 Corinthians 4:2. Note that the key word in this passage, as well as in our Lord's teachings, is not service, or labor, but faithfulness. Describe what the word *faithful* means to you.

____

____

Under the section on rewards, the author uses the term redemptive lift. Explain what this phrase means in terms of contemporary life. Review the redemptive lift principle in your own life or in the life of your parents or someone you know very well.

____

____

It seems quite obvious that stewardship impacts all our personal relationships. Set forth your relationship priorities. Now look at these relationships in light of the Great Commandment Chart and evaluate where you are. The objective is to avoid Satan's scheme and to fully adopt the New Testament strategy for faithful, victorious living.

____

____

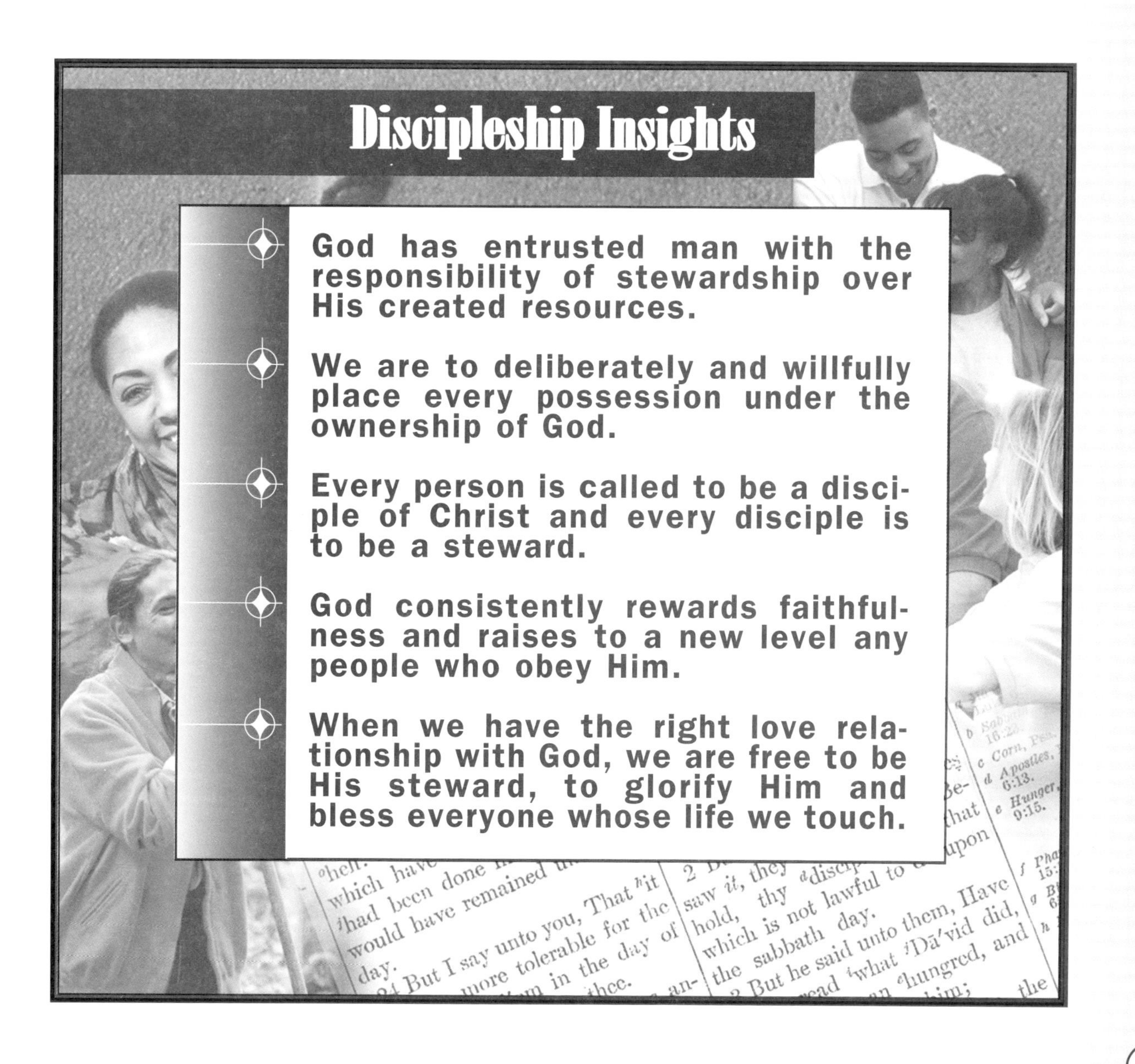

Resources

Gothard, Bill, *Men's Manual*, Volume 2. Institute in Basic Youth Conflicts.

Jackson, *Christianomics*. Winston Crown.

McAfee, Caleb, *Money and the Christian*. McAfee. Irvin, Texas

Taylor, Al, *Proving God*. Pathway Press. Cleveland, Tenn.

NOTES:

Winning Our World

Junus C. Fulbright

INTRODUCTION

In Hampton Court near London, England, there is a grapevine that is about 1,000 years old. The vine has but one root, which is at least two feet thick. Some of the branches are 200 feet long. The vine produces several tons of grapes each year. Even though some of the smaller branches are 200 feet from the main stem, they bear much fruit because they are joined to the vine and allow the life of the vine to flow into them.

Vine and Branches

Jesus said, "I am the vine, you are the branches. He who abides in Me, and I in him, bears much fruit; for without Me you can do nothing" (John 15:5). Jesus is the true vine; we are His branches. If we abide in Jesus, we—like the Hampton Court vine—also will bear much fruit. Our fruit bearing will glorify God and establish our discipleship: "By this My Father is glorified, that you bear much fruit; so you will be My disciples" (John 15:8).

Disciples Are *Doers*

Jesus makes it clear that disciples are not just followers. The Lord's disciples are *doers*. True disciples bear much fruit. In his letter to the Colossian Christians, the apostle Paul prayed that they would "walk worthy of the Lord, fully pleasing Him, being fruitful in every good work and increasing in the knowledge of God" (Colossians 1:10).

What fruit are disciples to bear? Obviously this includes the fruit of the Spirit (Galatians 5:22) as well other spiritual graces (Ephesians 5:9). However, the Greek word translated as *fruit* in John 15 is *karpos*, which means "to gather fruit into life eternal."

The emphasis of John 15 is on a *spiritual harvest*. Gathering fruit into eternal life is the reason Jesus came into the world: "For God so loved the world that He gave His only begotten Son, that whoever believes in Him should not perish but have everlasting life" (John 3:16). Because "He who says he abides in Him ought himself also to walk just as He walked" (1 John 2:6), the main focus of disciples should be winning others for the spiritual harvest.

Spiritual Harvest

Applying the Truth

MY DAILY WALK WITH GOD

Take a few moments to search your life and look for things that may hinder you from being a disciple who bears much fruit.

Ask yourself, "What do I need to do to assure that I am abiding in the vine?"

Set aside time for prayer during which you ask the Lord to help you be a fruitful disciple.

During His final days on earth Jesus gave commandments to the apostles through the Holy Spirit (Acts 1:2). One of these commandments has come to be known as the Great Commission.

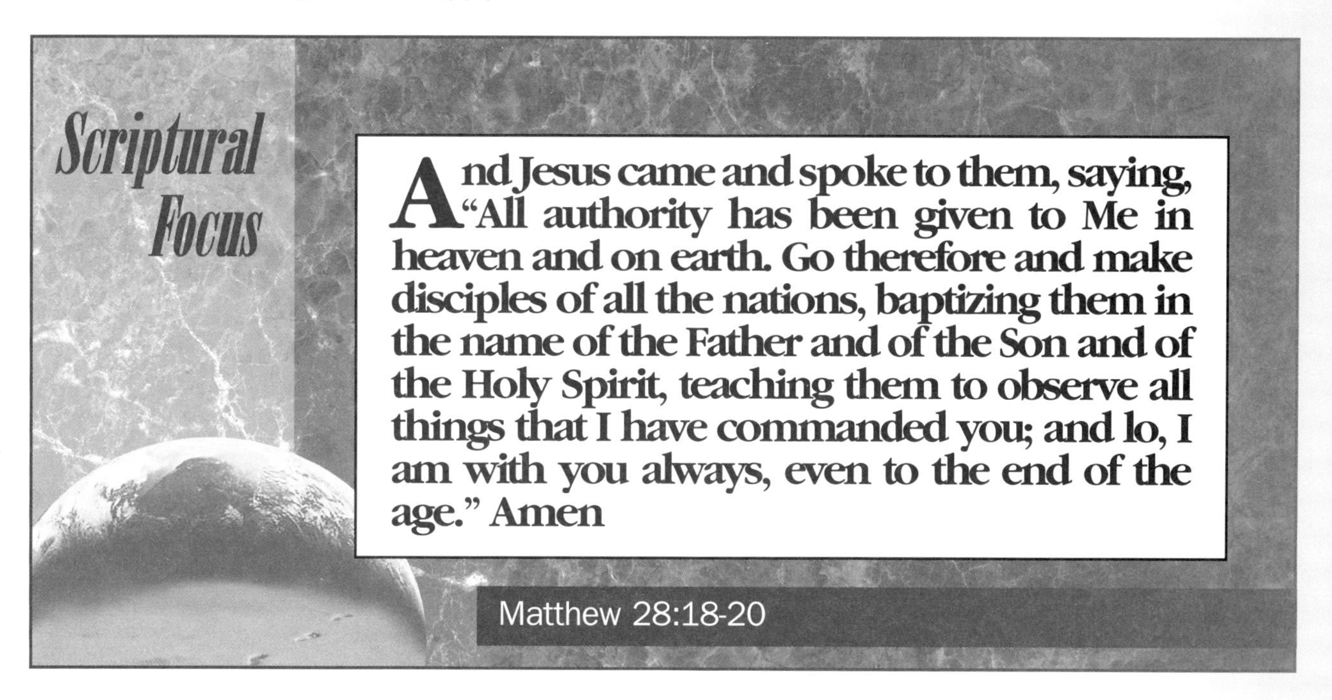

The Great Commission is the mission and message of the church. Across 20 centuries, the ageless message of salvation has passed unchanged from generation to generation. Methods have changed, but neither the mission nor

The Great Commission

the message has changed in the nearly 2,000 years since Jesus first charged His disciples to "make disciples of all the nations" (Matthew 28:19). Making disciples is still the primary responsibility of every child of God.

As Reinhard Bonnke has said:

> When the Lord appointed twelve men to be His first witnesses, He sent them out to introduce the Gospel to the world. Our task is to follow their lead. Today we tread where they led. Their distinction as apostles was to initiate all evangelism. Jesus gave them His teaching and they, in turn, gave it to us (*Evangelism by Fire*, p. 83).

EMPOWERED TO WIN OUR WORLD

Empowered to Witness

After charging His disciples with the responsibility for winning their world, Jesus told them that they would be empowered by the Holy Spirit to be witnesses for Him:

> Then He said to them, "Thus it is written, and thus it was necessary for the Christ to suffer and to rise from the dead the third day, and that repentance and remission of sins should be preached in His name to all nations, beginning at Jerusalem. And you are witnesses of these things. Behold, I send the Promise of My Father upon you; but tarry in the city of Jerusalem until you are endued with power from on high" (Luke 24:46-49).

Then, as Jesus prepared to return to heaven, He instructed His disciples to remain in Jerusalem after His ascension. They were to "wait for the Promise of the Father, 'which,' He said, 'you have heard from Me; for John truly baptized with water, but you shall be baptized with the Holy Spirit not many days from now'" (Acts 1:4, 5). Jesus also told them, " . . . you shall receive power when the Holy Spirit has come upon you; and you shall be witnesses to Me in Jerusalem, and in all Judea and Samaria, and to the end of the earth" (1:8).

Promise of the Holy Spirit

During His earthly ministry Jesus had promised the disciples that the Holy Spirit would come to them: "I will pray the Father, and he shall give you another Comforter, that he may abide with you for ever" (John 14:16). "The Comforter, which is the Holy Ghost, whom the Father will send in my name, he shall teach you all things, and bring all things to your remembrance, whatsoever I have said unto you" (John 14:26). "It is expedient for you that I go away: for if I go not away, the Comforter will not come unto you; but if I depart, I will send him unto you" (John 16:7).

Obedient to the Lord's commandment, the disciples waited in Jerusalem. The Scriptures record:

Obedience

> When the Day of Pentecost had fully come, they were all with one accord in one place. And suddenly there came a sound from heaven, as of a rushing mighty wind, and it filled the whole house where they were sitting. Then there appeared to them divided tongues, as of fire, and one sat upon each of them. And they were all filled with the Holy Spirit and began to speak with other tongues, as the Spirit gave them utterance (Acts 2:1-4).

Outpouring of the Holy Spirit

When news of the happenings at the Upper Room was noised abroad, a multitude soon gathered in amazement. Some of them questioned the meaning of the disciples' strange actions; others merely mocked and said they were drunk.

In answer to the charge of drunkenness, Peter said: "Men of Judea and all who dwell in Jerusalem, let this be known to you, and heed my words. For these are not drunk, as you suppose, since it is *only* the third hour of the day. But this is what was spoken by the prophet Joel" (Acts 2:14-16). The outpouring of the anointing Joel had foreseen 800 years before had come to pass! The power Jesus had promised His disciples had been given!

Holy Spirit Power

Why did the disciples need Holy Spirit power? Why was it so important that the Comforter come to them? Why were they to wait for the anointing from on high? The answer is that they had been given a supreme task that demanded a powerful presence. Jesus had commissioned them to win their world!

A Super-charged Church

When Jesus died on the cross, the disciples were discouraged and despondent. After Pentecost, they immediately became encouraged and empowered. What was the difference? The fire of God had fallen on them. Divinity had touched humanity and transformed the disciples. Suddenly they were a dynamo of spiritual power—an anointed assembly, a fire-baptized fellowship, a super-charged church!

Filling the Earth with the Gospel

Those who had been fearful and failing now proclaimed the gospel of Christ to their generation with Pentecostal boldness and "the Lord added to the church daily such as should be saved" (Acts 2:47). The disciples went forth ministering under the anointing of the Spirit, lifting up the Lord Jesus Christ and filling the earth with the gospel message. Churches were established throughout the Mediterranean world. The disciples' powerful Spirit-anointed witness changed their world so much that it was said of them that they had "turned the world upside down" (Acts 17:6).

Sometimes we may look at the phenomenal success of the early Christians and imagine that these world-changers were superhuman spiritual giants. However, the truth is they were ordinary men and women—common people—with uncommon resources, extraordinary reserves and supernatural power. What made their witnessing so effective was the anointing of the Holy Spirit that empowered them to win their world!

Applying the Truth

MY DAILY WALK WITH GOD

The Holy Spirit empowers us to win our world. The Holy Spirit baptism is necessary for effective witnessing.

Have you been filled with the Spirit? If not, take a few moments to reflect on things that may be hindering your receiving His fullness. Ask God to help you overcome them.

If you have been filled with the Spirit, ask the Lord to help you to be sensitive to the Spirit's leading.

COMMISSIONED TO WIN OUR WORLD

The Call of Every Disciple

We may be reluctant to even try to win souls because we believe we can never witness for Christ as effectively as the early Christians, but the truth is we have no choice in the matter. The Great Commission—Christ's charge to the church—is the responsibility of *every* disciple. Jesus said, " . . . you shall be witnesses to Me in Jerusalem, and in all Judea and Samaria, and to the end of the earth" (Acts 1:8). We *all* are called to win our world!

Reinhard Bonnke has said:

> A Christian is a witness. The name "Christian" was coined in early Antioch because it easily identified believers. They were the people who always talked about Christ. The Christian's business is not busyness, but witnessing. Witnessing is the commerce of the people of the kingdom of God (*Evangelism by Fire*, pp. 53, 54).

Anointing

Along with the responsibility to win our world comes an empowering anointing. Jesus said, "He dwells with you and will be in you" (John 14:17), and promised, "I will send Him to you" (John 16:7). As we witness to our world, God assures us, "My Presence will go with you" (Exodus 33:14). Although we may feel inadequate within ourselves, the Holy Spirit can do mighty works through us if we will yield ourselves to be used of the Lord.

EQUIPPED TO WIN OUR WORLD

21st Century Methods

Although the mission and the message of the church is unchangeable, methods must of necessity change. Methods that worked in past eras may not be as effective for the 21st century. It is inconceivable to think that Jesus and

Paul would not take advantage of today's multimedia technology in presenting their message if they were here today. The church should seize every opportunity to present the gospel in a manner that will reach today's high-tech, cyber-savvy generation.

A Higher Plane

In his book *The People Principle* (p. 94), Stan Toler says:

> The gospel never changes. Jesus Christ is the same yesterday, today, forever. Outreach methods *do* change, though. Those that worked in the '70s and '80s do not work anymore, and it is futile (and perhaps a bit vain) to insist on using outdated means to convey the good news of salvation. In their book *The Issachar Factor*, Gary McIntosh and Glen Martin have outlined what worked *then* and what works *now*:

Then and Now

That was then . . .	***This is now . . .***
Door-to-door	Friend-to-friend
Confrontational	Relational
Tracts	Multimedia
Hard Sell	Soft sell
Evangelism committees	Evangelism teams
Guilt-driven	Love-motivated
Evangelism as a duty	Outreach as a lifestyle

One-by-one Method

The best method for reaching people with the gospel today seems to be a personal, friend-to-friend, love-motivated approach. As Billy Graham has said:

> One of the first verses of Scripture that Dawson Trotman, founder of the Navigators, made me memorize was, "The things that thou hast heard of me among many witnesses, the same commit thou to faithful men, who shall be able to teach others also" (2 Timothy 2:2, KJV). This is a little like a mathematical formula for spreading the gospel and enlarging the church. Paul taught Timothy; Timothy shared what he knew with faithful men; these faithful men would then teach others also. And so the process goes on and on. If every believer followed this pattern, the church could reach the entire world with the gospel in one generation! Mass crusades, in which I believe and to which I have committed my life, will never finish the Great Commission; but a one-by-one ministry will" (*The Holy Spirit*, p. 147).

A PERSON-TO-PERSON PLAN

Personal Evangelism

One of the greatest joys in the disciple's life is leading someone else into discipleship. The apostle Paul voiced this when he wrote: "For what is our hope, or joy, or crown of rejoicing? Is it not even you in the presence of our Lord Jesus Christ at His coming?" (1 Thessalonians 2:19). It is important to learn how to lead someone to Christ and to be spiritually sensitive to the opportunities the Holy Spirit provides for witnessing to unsaved family members, friends, and co-workers. The individuals who are closest to us are in our circle of influence and are usually among the first people we will be able to reach with the gospel.

Stan Toler says:

> Personal evangelism is always a one-to-one relationship; effective only as we build bridges of kinship with the person we are leading to the throne. Jesus showed us this time and time again during His life, and we would be foolish to stray from His model. The message might be delivered en masse, but it is received only through person-to-person contact in a moment of sincere prayer (*The People Principle*, p. 88).

A FOUR-POINT PLAN FOR SOULWINNING

Four-step Method

✦ Pray

Toler has developed a four-step process that he calls The *ABCs of a Personal Relationship with Christ*. The first step in personal evangelism is to pray in advance for God's anointing as the gospel is presented. The second step is to present the plan of salvation to a friend or family member using three simple steps:

✦ Present the Plan of Salvation

1. **A**dmit that you have sinned (Romans 3:23).
2. **B**elieve that Jesus died for you (John 1:12).
3. **C**onfess that Jesus is Lord of your life (Romans 10:9, 10).

✦ Leading in the Sinner's Prayer

Toler's third step is to lead the person in a sinner's prayer. He suggests something like this: *Dear Lord Jesus, I know I'm a sinner. I believe that You died for my sins and rose from the grave. I now turn from my sins and invite You to come into my heart and life. I receive You as my personal Savior and follow You as my Lord. Amen.*

This prayer can be committed to memory and recited, with the person being lead to the Lord repeating it.

✦ Assure the New Convert

The fourth step in Toler's plan is to assure the new convert that what has happened is real and true. Toler suggests 1 John 5:11, 12, as verses of assurance: *And this is the testimony: that God has given us eternal life, and this life is in His Son. He who has the Son has life; he who does not have the Son of God does not have life.* These Scriptures, too, can be committed to memory for use during the witnessing session.

FOLLOW-UP IS ESSENTIAL FOR MAKING DISCIPLES

The Goal *Make Disciples*

"The process of evangelizing is not complete until those who have responded to the claims of Christ are active, functioning members of the local church," says Toler. "In other words, the goal of evangelism is not just to get a decision—it is to make disciples" (*The People Principle*, p. 105).

In *Your Ministry of Evangelism*, Elmer L. Towns said:

> Jesus commissioned His followers to "make disciples," not simply to make decisions. The decision to receive Christ as Savior is the beginning of a life of discipleship. If God gives you an

opportunity to lead someone to Christ, you will want to help that person grow as a Christian. Your initial follow-up of this new believer begins even before you part company after presenting the gospel (pp. 39, 49).

Follow-up Process

Towns suggests a three-point follow-up process:

1. Be sure the person understands what has happened.
2. Invite the person to attend church with you.
3. Continue nurturing the person in discipleship.

Applying the Truth

MY DAILY WALK WITH GOD

Make a list of several unsaved individuals—family, friends, or co-workers—who are a part of your circle of influence.

____

____

____

____

____

Pray for their salvation each day. Also, pray that the Holy Spirit will give you opportunities to witness to them.

LESSON REVIEW

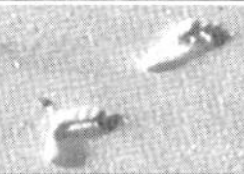

Jesus calls his disciples to bear much fruit, which they cannot do unless they abide in Him. Bearing fruit means "to gather fruit into life eternal." The main focus of disciples should be winning others for the spiritual harvest. The Great Commission—"make disciples of all nations"—is the mission and message of the church, and the primary responsibility of every child of God. Jesus called us to win *our* world—our circle of influence—and He empowered us by the Holy Spirit to be witnesses. Although we may feel inadequate in ourselves, the Holy Spirit can do mighty works through us if we will yield ourselves to the lordship of Christ. The best method for reaching people today is a personal, friend-to-friend, love-motivated approach. Converts should be affirmed through followed-up and nurtured into fruitful discipleship.

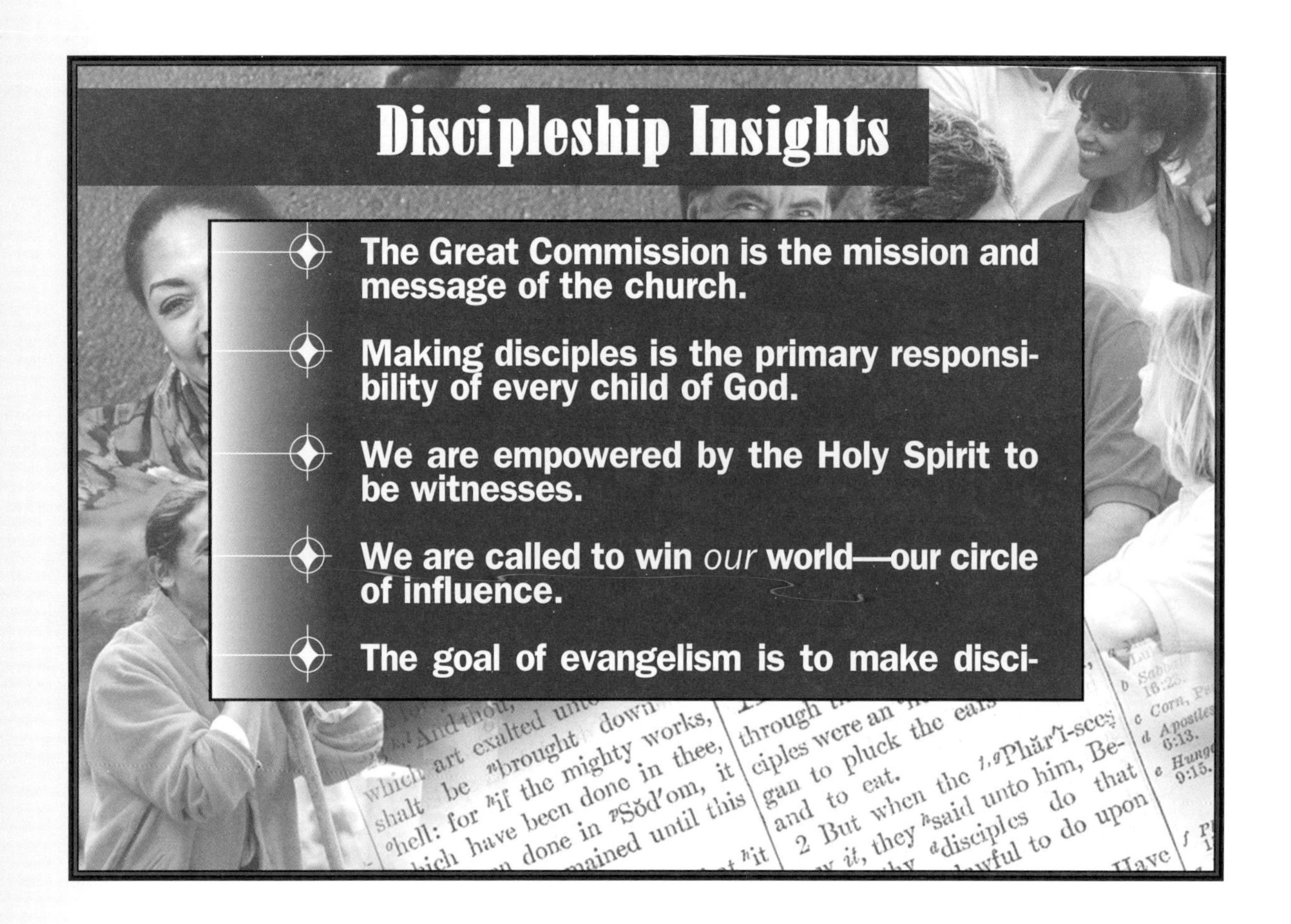

RESOURCES

Bonnke, Reinhard. *Evangelism by Fire: Igniting Your Passion for the Lost*. Dallas, Texas: Word Publishing, 1990.

Bright, Vonette, Ball, Barbara. *The Joy of Hospitality: Fun Ideas for Evangelistic Entertaining*. Orlando, Florida: NewLife Publications, 1996.

Graham, Billy. *The Holy Spirit*. Waco, Texas: Word, 1978.

Toler, Stan. *The People Principle: Transforming Laypersons into Leaders*. Kansas City, Missouri: Beacon Hill Press of Kansas City, 1997.

Towns, Elmer L. *Your Ministry of Evangelism: A Guide for Church Volunteers*. Wheaton, Illinois: Evangelical Training Association, 1991.

Walking With Jesus

Tom George

INTRODUCTION

"Lifestyle" is a 20th-century word that by definition is "the typical way of life of an individual, group, or culture." Lifestyle almost always is used in connection with a descriptive adjective—*secular* lifestyle, *alternative* lifestyle, *traditional* lifestyle, and so forth—and involves adherence to a particular way of life. Secular lifestyle describes a way of life that excludes religion. Alternative lifestyle most frequently refers to a way of life based on a non-heterosexual sexual orientation. Traditional lifestyle usually reflects a Judeo-Christian view of life.

Devotion to Christ

Jesus said, "I have come that they may have life, and that they may have it more abundantly" (John 10:10). Accepting Christ as Savior implies adherence to a Christian view of life that is not so much devotion to a set of principles as it is a devotion to a person. Jesus Christ does not call us to devote ourselves to a cause or a creed; he asks us to devote ourselves to Him. Our devotion to Christ is lived out in our daily Christian walk. We call this a *Christian lifestyle*.

"Christianity," said imminent theologian William Barclay, "is something which is meant to be seen. As someone has well said, 'There can be no such thing as secret discipleship, for either the secrecy destroys the discipleship, or the discipleship destroys the secrecy.' A man's Christianity should be perfectly visible to all men."

Christianity Is Visible

If, as Barclay says, Christianity should be visible, the best way to demonstrate it is through a Christian lifestyle that is an open expression of our daily walk with Christ. As John the apostle stated, "He who says he abides in Him ought himself also to walk just as He walked" (1 John 2:6). "Walking" (Greek, *peripateo*) is a metaphor for "living" or "conducting one's life."

How does a Christian conduct his life? How is a Christian lifestyle different from a secular lifestyle? What are the characteristics of a Christian lifestyle? These are some of the questions we will examine in this lesson.

It should be emphasized that the path to a Christian lifestyle is not found through earning spiritual points or subscribing to asceticism. Living a Christian lifestyle does not depend on what we do or do not do as much as on what Christ does in us.

The apostle Paul expressed the essence of the Christian lifestyle in his writings to the church in Galatia . . . .

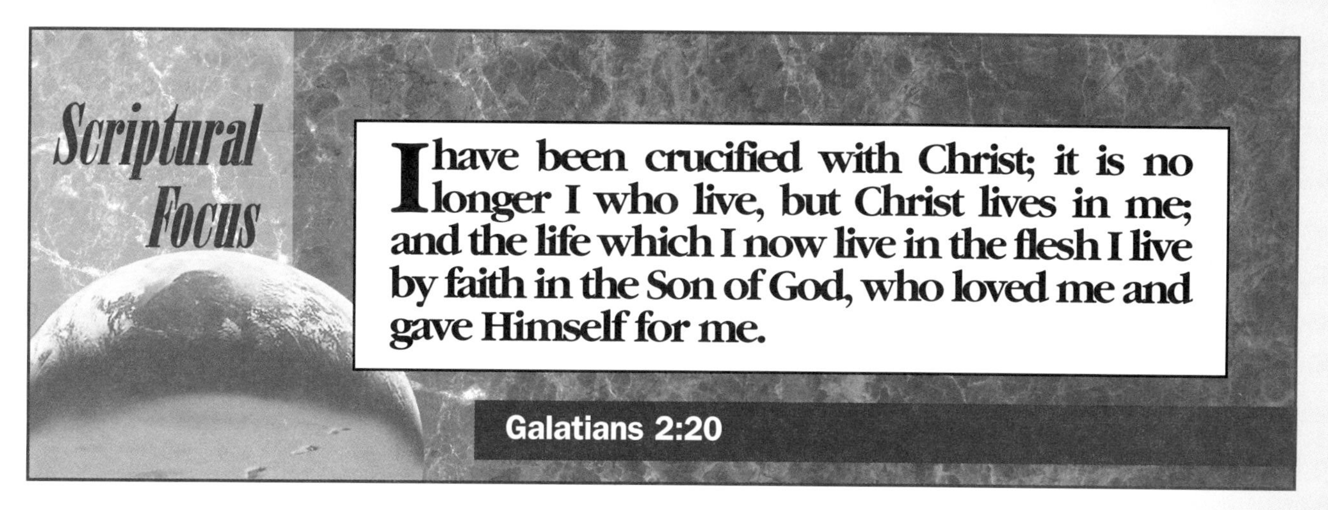

Spiritually Resurrected

When we accept Jesus as our Savior, we are crucified with Him in a spiritual sense. Our old unregenerate life dies and we are spiritually resurrected to a new life in Jesus Christ. We no longer live as we formerly did, but Christ lives in us. From that time forward our earthly life is to be lived by faith in Jesus.

Dietrich Bonhoeffer, the German theologian who was executed by the Nazis, said, "When Christ calls a man, He bids him come and die." Most of us will never be expected to suffer physical death for our testimony. However, in order for us to live a Christian lifestyle, sin and self must die and Jesus must become Lord of our lives.

Total Spiritual Commitment

Paul described the Christian experience as a walk. However, walking with Jesus is not a haphazard journey; it is a lifelong odyssey of excellence that requires a total spiritual commitment to the lordship of Jesus Christ.

Under the lordship of Christ, we indeed walk in a new way and are no longer slave to the sins of the past, as Paul pointed out in his letter to the Roman Christians:

> Therefore we were buried with Him through baptism into death, that just as Christ was raised from the dead by the glory of the Father, even so we also should walk in newness of life. For if we have been united together in the likeness of His death, certainly we also shall be in the likeness of His resurrection, knowing this, that our old man was crucified with Him, that the body of sin might be done away with, that we should no longer be slaves of sin (Romans 6:4-6).

The Christian lifestyle is a walk of faith that is committed to Christ, centered in the Word of God, and led by the Holy Spirit.

A COMMITTED WALK

We Belong to God

"Committed" (Greek, *paradidomee*) means "to give into the hands of another." When we accept the Lord, we give ourselves into His hands and commit our lives to His will and direction. We are His because Jesus purchased our salvation with His sacrifice at Calvary. Paul told the Corinthians believers that both the body and spirit belong to God: "For you were bought at a price; therefore glorify God in your body and in your spirit, which are God's" (1 Corinthians 6:20).

COMMITMENT IS A CONSCIOUS DECISION

Directed by the Lord

Christian commitment is a conscious decision to voluntarily surrender oneself into the Lord's hands. Not only do we give ourselves into His hands, we also give ourselves into His power and use. Our decision to surrender ourselves to the Lord is the first step in a lifelong walk with Him.

The committed walk is a journey directed by the Lord. The psalmist declared: "The steps of a good man are ordered by the Lord, and He delights in his way. Though he fall, he shall not be utterly cast down; for the Lord upholds him with His hand" (Psalm 37:23, 24).

Applying the Truth

MY DAILY WALK WITH GOD

List ways the Lord has directed your spiritual walk.

____

____

____

____

____

WE ARE TO FOLLOW JESUS

The prophet Jeremiah understood the frailties of mankind and recognized our need to be committed to the Lord's direction for spiritual wellbeing.

Jeremiah declared: "O Lord, I know the way of man is not in himself; it is not in man who walks to direct his own steps" (Jeremiah 10:23).

Jesus Is Our Shepherd

If the way of man is not in himself, then it naturally follows that we must look beyond ourselves. The way, said the apostle Peter, is Jesus Christ: "For to this you were called, because Christ also suffered for us, leaving us an example, that you should follow His steps" (1 Peter 2:21). When we commit our way to Jesus and follow His steps, we die to sin and live for righteousness and, though we once were "like sheep going astray," Jesus becomes the "Shepherd and Overseer" of our souls (1 Peter 2:24, 25).

Our existence has an eternal purpose and our lives fit into God's divine plan. When we commit our lives to Jesus, He will be the Shepherd and Overseer of our souls on every step of our spiritual journey with Him. The Lord directs our walk through both the written Word of God and the guidance of the Holy Spirit, as we will see further in this lesson.

A WORD-CENTERED WALK

The Bible Is Our Map

It would be difficult to go on a trip without a map to show the way. We also need a map to guide us on our spiritual journey. The Christian's map is the Bible—the eternal Word of God.

The Bible is composed of 66 books in two divisions—the Old Testament and the New Testament. The Old Testament contains 39 books written by 28 authors. It begins with the Creation in Genesis 1:1 and tells the story of God's relationship with His people up the time of Christ. The New Testament contains 27 books written by nine authors. It begins with the birth of Jesus, and tells of His life and ministry, and the ministry of the early church and the apostles. However, the Bible is far more than just another book. It is the Christian's infallible guidebook—God's directive for our spiritual walk.

GOD'S WORD IS A GUIDEBOOK FOR CHRISTIAN LIVING

Although much of the Bible is a historical record of God's relationship with His people, the narrative is interspersed with many practical lessons. These lessons illustrate both the folly of sin and the reward of faith. Thus, the Bible serves as a guidebook for the child of God in all situations of life.

Hiding the Word in Our Hearts

The psalmist David understood how important knowledge of the Word of God is to our spiritual walk. He told God, "Your word I have hidden in my heart, that I might not sin against You!" (Psalm 119:11). His prayer was, "Direct my steps by Your word, and let no iniquity have dominion over me" (Psalm 119:133). Our Christian walk is much easier when the Word becomes a part of us. As the psalmist said, "The law of his God is in his heart; none of his steps shall slide" (Psalm 37:31).

Applying the Truth

MY DAILY WALK WITH GOD

Fill in the blanks with the correct word or words. Answers can be found in the lesson.

Paul described the Christian experience as a ________.

______________ means "to give into the hands of another."

Christian commitment is a ____________ decision.

The Christian's ____________ is the Bible.

The Christian lifestyle is a ______________________ that is

__________________________, __________________________,

and ________________________________.

Answers: 1. Walk 2. Committed 3. Conscious 4. Map 5. Walk of faith; committed to Christ; centered in the Word of God; led by the Holy Spirit.

THE BIBLE IS AN INFALLIBLE GUIDE

The Word Is Proven

In times of trial or uncertainty, the child of God can draw on the lessons of the Bible for spiritual direction. The Word of God has stood the test of time. Through the ages, multitudes have testified to the Bible's sustaining power in their lives. God's Word is a dependable, proven, and unfailing guidebook for life: "As for God, His way is perfect; the word of the Lord is proven; He is a shield to all who trust in Him" (Psalm 18:30). A regular time of Bible reading and meditation on the Word should be a part of every Christian's daily walk with God.

A Christian lifestyle is lived in and by the Word of God for "Man shall not live by bread alone, but by every word of God" (Luke 4:4). A Christian lifestyle is also lived in the Holy Spirit, as we will see in the next section.

A SPIRIT-LED WALK

The Holy Spirit Is Our Guide

A journey is much easier if we have a guide—someone who can show us the way. Our guide for the Christian walk is the Holy Spirit. Paul, writing to the Roman Christians, said, "For as many as are led by the Spirit of God, these are sons of God" (Romans 8:14).

CHRISTIANS WALK IN THE POWER OF THE SPIRIT

Our Christian walk must be lived in the power of the Holy Spirit if we are to be effective witnesses of Christ. Christians do not walk in the way of the world but according to the leading of the Spirit. Paul said, "There is therefore now no condemnation to those who are in Christ Jesus, who do not walk according to the flesh, but according to the Spirit" (Romans 8:1).

A Higher Plane

Walking "according to the Spirit" is on a higher plane than the way of the world. Christians have a different set of values: "For those who live according to the flesh set their minds on the things of the flesh, but those who live according to the Spirit, the things of the Spirit" (Romans 8:5). While the world is obsessed with "the things of the flesh," Christians "live according to the Spirit" and are motivated not by the values of the world, but by "the things of the Spirit."

In *A Layman's Guide to the Fruit of the Spirit*, T. David Sustar wrote:

> A spiritual person is not so much a person possessing a strong spiritual character as he is a person filled with the Holy Spirit. The glory of the new creation is not only that the human spirit is recreated, but it also fits it for the abode of God himself and makes it dependent upon Him for its life. The highest spirituality, therefore, is that crucified life, entirely dependent upon and completely empowered by the Holy Spirit (p. 126).

LIFE IN THE SPIRIT IS ABUNDANT LIFE

Abounding In Blessings

Jesus came to give us abundant life (John 10:10). That "abundance" is fully realized by living in the Holy Spirit: "Now may the God of hope fill you with all joy and peace in believing, that you may abound in hope by the power of the Holy Spirit" (Romans 15:13). Joy, peace, and hope—in abundance—belong to the child of God who walks in the power of the Holy Spirit.

The difference that living in the Spirit and being led by the Spirit makes in our Christian walk will be evident not only in our relationship with God but also in our relationship with other people. After Pentecost, the Spirit-led church had "favor with all the people" (Acts 2:47). "Favor" (Greek, *charis*) means "grace" or "good will." A life lived in the Spirit brings grace to our relationships with all people.

AN HONORABLE WALK

Walking Worthy

A lifestyle that is committed to Christ, directed by the Word of God, and led by the Holy Spirit is an honorable walk that glorifies God and is a constant witness for Him. Paul prayed that the Colossian Christians would "walk worthy of the Lord, fully pleasing Him, being fruitful in every good work and increasing in the knowledge of God" (Colossians 1:10).

Living Peaceably

In a world of fractured relationships, broken promises, conflict, and mistrust, it is good to remember Paul's admonition to the Romans: "If it is possible, as much as depends on you, live peaceably with all men" (Romans 12:18).

Living "peaceably with all men" implies more than just a proper relationship with our fellow Christians. The early Christians had "favor with all the people" (Acts 2:47). If our lifestyle is to be a witness for the Lord, it must witness to "all the people," not just other Christians.

A CHRISTIAN LIFESTYLE IS CENTERED IN RELATIONSHIPS

Christian Conduct

A Christian lifestyle is centered in a proper relationship with God and with people. A right relationship with God in Jesus Christ is prerequisite to right relationships with people. We develop a right relationship with God by committing ourselves to Christ, by making the Bible our guide for conduct, and by being sensitive to the leading of the Holy Spirit. We cultivate right relationships with other people by living a consistent Christian lifestyle.

Applying the Truth

MY DAILY WALK WITH GOD

"But now you yourselves are to put off all these: anger, wrath, malice, blasphemy, filthy language out of your mouth. Do not lie to one another, since you have put off the old man with his deeds, and have put on the new man who is renewed in knowledge according to the image of Him who created him. . . . Therefore, as the elect of God, holy and beloved, put on tender mercies, kindness, humility, meekness, longsuffering; bearing with one another, and forgiving one another, if anyone has a complaint against another; even as Christ forgave you, so you also must do. But above all these things put on love, which is the bond of perfection. And let the peace of God rule in your hearts, to which also you were called in one body; and be thankful" (Colossians 3:8-15).

Take a sheet of paper and write the heading "A Model for Christian Conduct" at the top. Just below the heading make two columns. Head one column "Put Off" and the other column "Put On." Read Colossians 3:8-15. List on your paper the things that are to be "put off" and the things that are to be "put on."

Is there anything on the list you still need to "put off?"________

____

____

What do you still need to "put on?"________________

____

____

CHARACTERISTICS OF A CHRISTIAN LIFESTYLE

Fruit of the Spirit

T. David Sustar listed these characteristics of a Christian lifestyle in *A Layman's Guide to the Fruit of the Spirit*. Sustar said:

> The Holy Spirit also enables us to live victoriously, fostering our Christian growth, enabling us to witness and empowering us for service.
>
> If we live in the Spirit, we will walk in the Spirit in . . .
>
> 1. **Love**—that has all the qualities of 1 Corinthians 13:1-13.
> 2. **Joy**—that is full of faith and rejoicing.
> 3. **Peace**—from the fact that sins are forgiven and we are whole, sound and complete in Christ.
> 4. **Longsuffering**—patience and forbearing that will surprise ourselves.
> 5. **Gentleness**—kindness and tenderness which at times may require helping the less fortunate.
> 6. **Goodness**—a reflection of the moral qualities of God in truth and righteousness.
> 7. **Faith**—faithfulness to duty which will one day bring a "Well done, thou good and faithful servant," from the Lord.
> 8. **Meekness**—controlled strength, like that of Christ and Moses; power to get the job done with gentleness.
> 9. **Temperance**—all thoughts, words, impulses and actions under the control of the Holy Spirit (p. 128).

Wisdom from Above

The fruit of the Spirit is always evident in a lifestyle that is committed to Christ. A committed lifestyle grows out of a right relationship with God and seeks always to live peaceably with others. The apostle James described this lifestyle as "wisdom that is from above." James said, "But the wisdom that is from above is first pure, then peaceable, gentle, willing to yield, full of mercy and good fruits, without partiality and without hypocrisy. Now the fruit of righteousness is sown in peace by those who make peace" (James 3:17, 18).

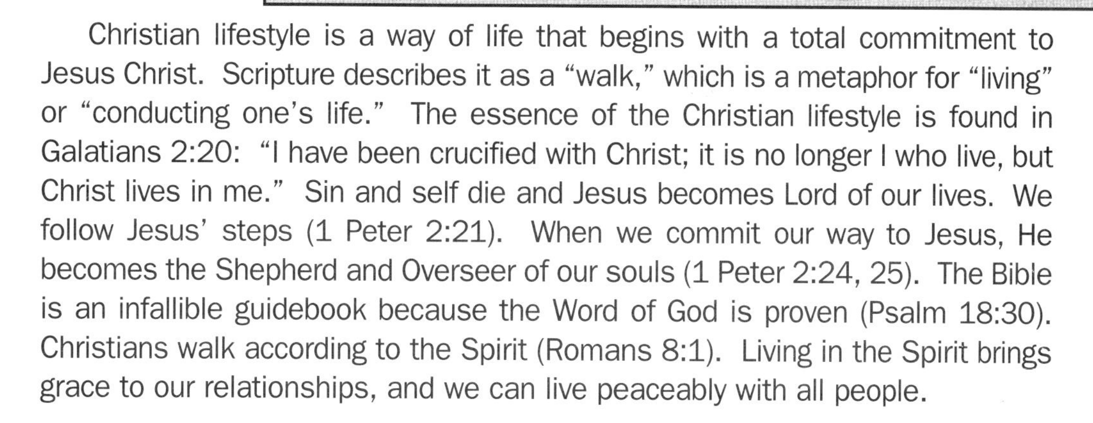

LESSON REVIEW

Christian lifestyle is a way of life that begins with a total commitment to Jesus Christ. Scripture describes it as a "walk," which is a metaphor for "living" or "conducting one's life." The essence of the Christian lifestyle is found in Galatians 2:20: "I have been crucified with Christ; it is no longer I who live, but Christ lives in me." Sin and self die and Jesus becomes Lord of our lives. We follow Jesus' steps (1 Peter 2:21). When we commit our way to Jesus, He becomes the Shepherd and Overseer of our souls (1 Peter 2:24, 25). The Bible is an infallible guidebook because the Word of God is proven (Psalm 18:30). Christians walk according to the Spirit (Romans 8:1). Living in the Spirit brings grace to our relationships, and we can live peaceably with all people.

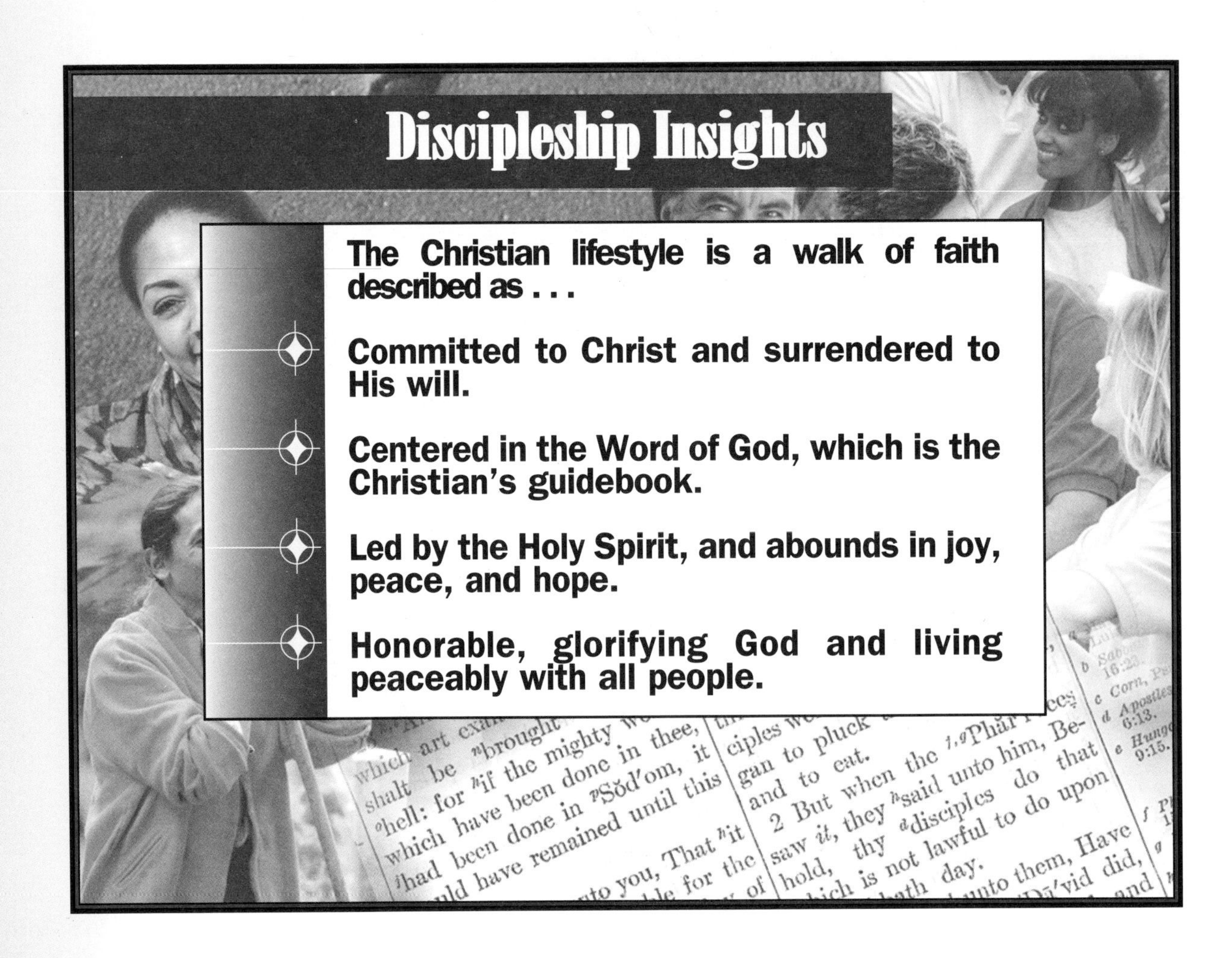

RESOURCES

Anders, Max E., *30 Days to Understanding the Bible*. Cleveland, Tenn.: Pathway Press, 1989.

Sustar, T. David, *A Layman's Guide to the Fruit of the Spirit*. Cleveland, Tenn.: Pathway Press, 1990.

Walker, Paul, *How to Keep Your Joy*. Nashville, Tenn.: Thomas Nelson, Inc., 1987

NOTES: ______________________________

____

____

____

____

____

EMPOWERED

Be Filled With the Holy Spirit

Daniel E. Black

INTRODUCTION

The Bible identifies the Holy Spirit as the Spirit of God and the Spirit of Christ. Therefore, when the Bible commands Christians to be filled with the Holy Spirit, that command is the same as saying, *Be filled with the Spirit of God* or *Be filled with the Spirit of Christ*. If we are filled with God's Spirit we will be godly; and if we are filled with Christ's Spirit we will be Christlike. When the Spirit-filled life is viewed from this perspective, it is perfectly normal for the Christian to want to be filled with the Holy Spirit.

Scriptural Focus

But you are not in the flesh [you are not living according to the desires of the sinful nature] but in the Spirit [but according to the desires of the Holy Spirit], if indeed the Spirit of God dwells in you. Now if anyone does not have the Spirit of Christ, he is not His.

Romans 8:9

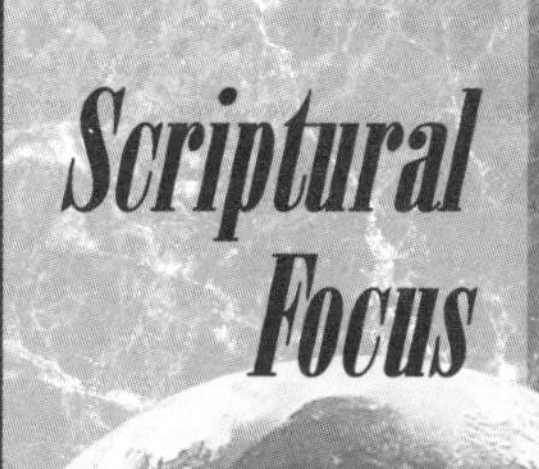

But you were washed [cleansed of your sins], but you were sanctified [consecrated to God], but you were justified [made right with God] in the name of the Lord Jesus and by the Spirit of our God.

1 Corinthians 6:11

THE HOLY SPIRIT IN YOUR LIFE

The Holy Spirit in Every Aspect of Life

To appreciate what it means to be filled with the Holy Spirit, first, you need to recognize that the Holy Spirit is involved in every aspect of your life as a Christian. Before you were a Christian, the Holy Spirit convinced you that you needed Christ as your Savior, and He persuaded you to come to Christ for salvation (John 16:7-11). When you came to Christ to be saved, you were cleansed of your sins, consecrated to God, and given a new spiritual life by the working of the Holy Spirit (John 3:5; Titus 3:5). Now, you have access to God by the Holy Spirit (Ephesians 2:18), and your entire life as a Christian is a new life "according to the Spirit" (Romans 8:1).

Regeneration

When you became a Christian, the Holy Spirit came into your life by regeneration (the new birth, being born again). By means of regeneration, the Holy Spirit, the Spirit of Christ, dwells in you. In fact, as the Bible says, "if anyone does not have the Spirit of Christ, he is not His" (Romans 8:9). It is not possible to be a Christian without having the Holy Spirit present in your life.

Filled With the Holy Spirit

When you think about being filled with the Holy Spirit, start with the fact that the Holy Spirit is present in your life right now. Recall all that He has already done to make you the Christian you are today. To be filled with the Spirit means His presence and power will become even more real and more effective in your life. To be filled with the Spirit means you will allow Him to have more control over your life.

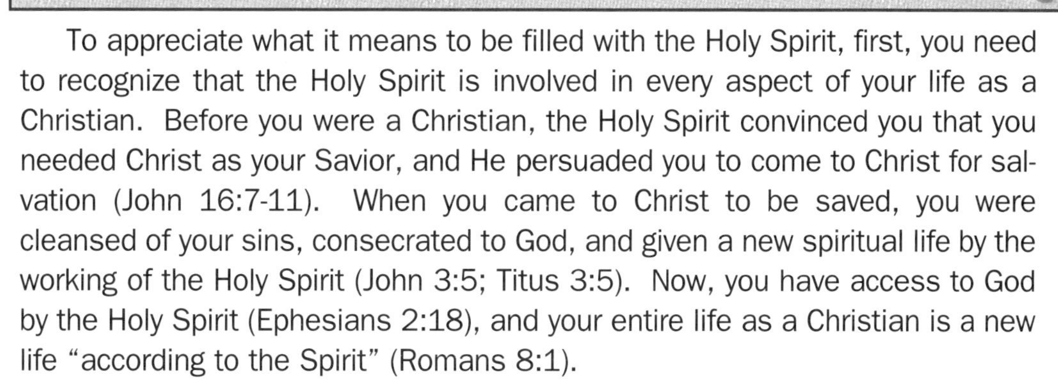

Applying the Truth

MY DAILY WALK WITH GOD

In what ways have you already experienced the presence of the

Holy Spirit in your life?________________________________

____

____

____

Thank God now for the presence of His Holy Spirit, the Spirit of Christ in your life, enabling you to be a Christian.

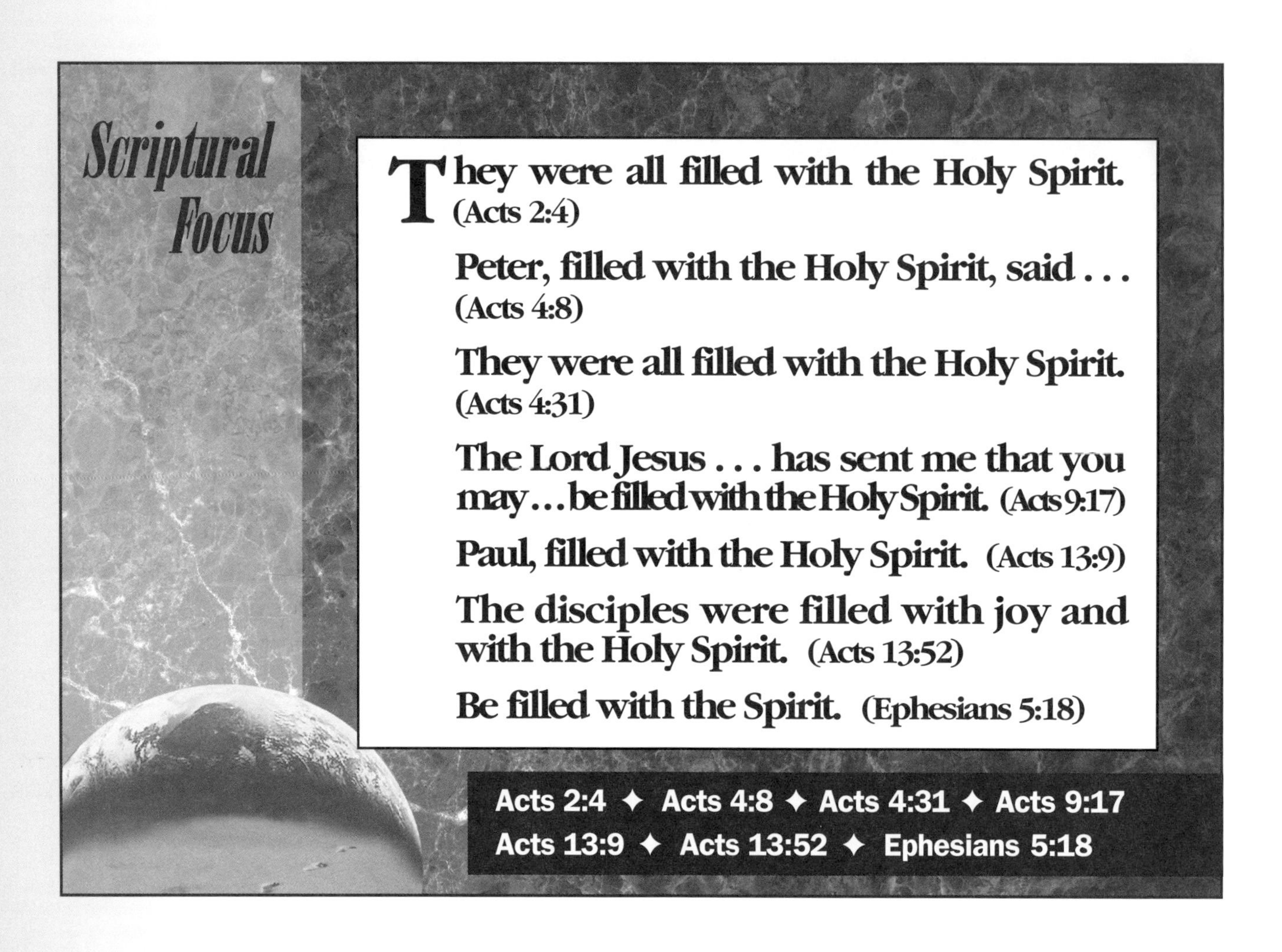

SPIRIT-FILLED LIVING IS COMMANDED

Early Church

In the early church the Spirit-filled life was regarded as the normal Christian life. Every believer in Christ was expected to be filled with the Holy Spirit. The apostle Paul was filled with the Spirit and he encouraged other Christians to be filled with the Spirit. In fact, in his letter to the Christians at Ephesus, Paul commanded them to be filled with the Spirit.

Four Rules

In the Greek language in which the New Testament was written, there are four rules regarding the use of verbs which lead us to four important truths about the command to "be filled" with the Spirit, recorded in Ephesians 5:18. Verbs have mood, tense, number, and voice. Each of these reveals a different aspect of the Greek verb for "be filled."

✦ A Commandment

First, the verb is in the imperative mood, meaning this is a command. Paul commanded Christians to be filled with the Spirit, and that commandment is still in force today. It is no less essential for Christians today to be filled with the Holy Spirit than it was in the time of the first Christians.

✦ Continuous Action

Second, the verb is in the present progressive tense. This means continuous action. A literal translation of this command could be something like this: "Be always being filled with the Spirit." Being filled with the Holy Spirit is not a one-time experience. It is, in fact, a continual, ongoing experience for the Christian.

✦ Everyone Be Filled

Third, the verb is in the plural number. This means "all of you" be filled with the Spirit. The command to be filled with the Spirit is not directed only to church leaders or a few choice members of the congregation. It is God's will for all Christians to be filled with His Holy Spirit.

✦ God Fills Us With His Spirit

Fourth, the verb is in the passive voice. This means the subject of the verb is not acting but being acted upon. That is, being filled with the Spirit is not something we can attain by our own efforts alone. Only God can fill us with His Spirit, and this is something we must rely on Him to do for us. However, God desires to fill us with His Spirit, and He will do this because we are believers in Christ. Through prayer, faith in God, and obedience to God's will (Matthew 21:22; Acts 5:32), we can be filled with the Holy Spirit.

Applying the Truth

MY DAILY WALK WITH GOD

Each of the following statements express the wrong attitude regarding the Spirit-filled life. What is wrong with these attitudes? What would be the right attitude in each case? (Write your answer after each statement.)

- Pastors and other church leaders need to be filled with the Holy Spirit, but that is not for me.______________________

____

- The Scriptural command to be filled with the Spirit does not apply to Christians today. ______________________________

____

If God wants to fill me with His Spirit He can, but I am satisfied just to know I am a Christian. ______________________

____

Scriptural Focus

And being assembled together with them [the disciples], He [Jesus] commanded them not to depart from Jerusalem, but to wait for the Promise of the Father, "which," He said, "you have heard from Me; for John truly baptized with water, but you shall be baptized with the Holy Spirit not many days from now." (Acts 1:4, 5)

When the Day of Pentecost had fully come, they were all with one accord in one place. And suddenly there came a sound from heaven, as of a rushing mighty wind, and it filled the whole house where they were sitting. Then there appeared to them divided tongues, as of fire, and one sat upon each of them. And they were all filled with the Holy Spirit and began to speak with other tongues, as the Spirit gave them utterance. (Acts 2:1-4)

When the apostles in Jerusalem heard that Samaria had accepted the word of God, they sent Peter and John to them. When they arrived, they prayed for them that they might receive the Holy Spirit, because the Holy Spirit had not yet come upon any of them; they had simply been baptized into the name of the Lord Jesus. Then Peter and John placed their hands on them, and they received the Holy Spirit. (Acts 8:14-17)

Acts 1:4, 5 ✦ Acts 2:1-4 ✦ Acts 8:14-17

BAPTISM IN THE SPIRIT AND FULLNESS OF THE SPIRIT

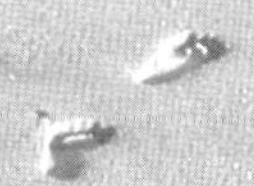

Baptism in the Holy Spirit

In the New Testament, the initial or beginning experience of being filled with the Holy Spirit is identified as the baptism in (with) the Holy Spirit. Jesus told His disciples that they would be baptized in the Holy Spirit. When, on the Day of Pentecost, they received that promised baptism in the Spirit, the Scripture says "they were all filled with the Holy Spirit" (Acts 2:4).

After the outpouring of the Holy Spirit on the Day of Pentecost, the Christians understood there was a distinct difference between the indwelling of the Holy Spirit received by regeneration (the new birth) and the fullness of the Spirit received by the baptism in the Spirit.

Samaria

That the early Christians recognized the fullness of the Spirit as different from and complementary to regeneration is apparent from the description of what happened to the converts in Samaria. They believed the gospel and were baptized in water, signifying their regeneration by faith in Christ. But still, they had not received the Holy Spirit as on the Day of Pentecost. But then, when Peter and John came to Samaria, and laid hands on the new converts and prayed for them to receive the Holy Spirit, they were baptized in, or filled with, the Holy Spirit.

Spirit-filled Living

Baptism in the Spirit is the beginning of the Spirit-filled life. After a Christian is baptized in the Spirit, it is necessary to maintain Spirit-filled living by continual faith, devotion, and obedience to Christ. Christians who take for granted that they will always be filled with the Spirit, because they have received the baptism in the Spirit, will not live Spirit-filled lives. But those who, after receiving the baptism in the Spirit, pray daily for the fullness of the Spirit in their lives, will be filled with the Spirit continually.

Applying the Truth

MY DAILY WALK WITH GOD

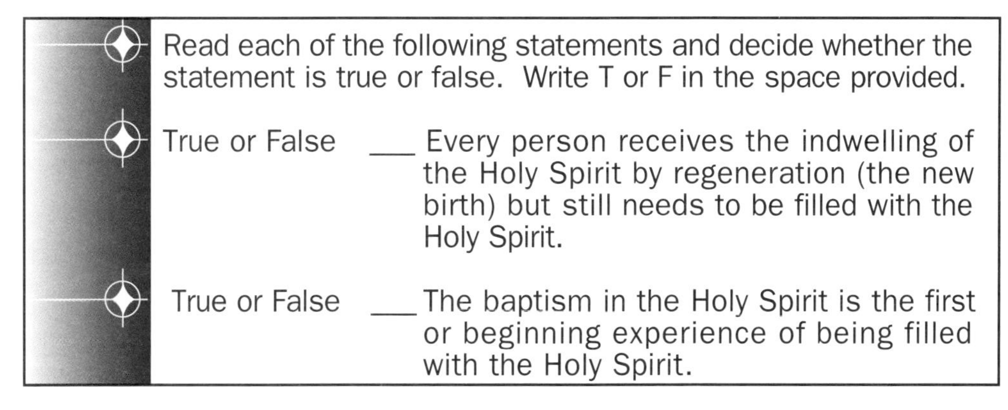

Read each of the following statements and decide whether the statement is true or false. Write T or F in the space provided.

True or False ___ Every person receives the indwelling of the Holy Spirit by regeneration (the new birth) but still needs to be filled with the Holy Spirit.

True or False ___ The baptism in the Holy Spirit is the first or beginning experience of being filled with the Holy Spirit.

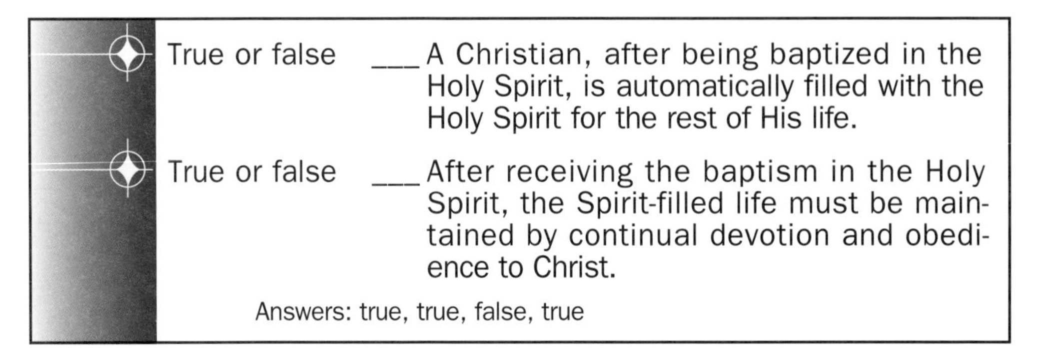

True or false ___ A Christian, after being baptized in the Holy Spirit, is automatically filled with the Holy Spirit for the rest of His life.

True or false ___ After receiving the baptism in the Holy Spirit, the Spirit-filled life must be maintained by continual devotion and obedience to Christ.

Answers: true, true, false, true

Scriptural Focus

But you shall receive power [spiritual enabling] when the Holy Spirit has come upon you; and you shall be witnesses . . . to the end of the earth. (Acts 1:8)

They were all filled with the Holy Spirit, and they spoke the word of God with boldness. . . . And great grace was upon them all. (Acts 4:31, 33)

I say then: Walk in the Spirit, and you shall not fulfill the lust of the flesh [and you will not obey the desires of the sinful nature]. . . . The fruit [harvest, produce, wealth] of the [Holy] Spirit [in your life] is love, joy, peace, longsuffering, kindness, goodness, faithfulness, gentleness, self-control. (Galatians 5:16, 22, 23)

Acts 1:8 ✦ Acts 4:31,33 ✦ Galatians 5:16, 22, 23

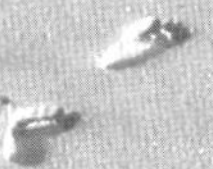

RESULTS OF BEING FILLED WITH THE SPIRIT

Initial Evidence

On the Day of Pentecost, the initial (first) outward evidence that the disciples of Jesus were filled with the Holy Spirit was that they "began to speak with other tongues, as the Spirit gave them utterance" (Acts 2:4). That initial evidence of the baptism in the Holy Spirit has been repeated in the lives of hundreds of millions who have been filled with the Holy Spirit. However, the goal of being filled with the

Holy Spirit is not to speak with tongues but to reflect the character of Christ and do the ministry of Christ in such a way that we will, in fact, become His witnesses.

Witnesses of Christ

Jesus said the fullness of the Spirit will enable us to "be" His witnesses. Testifying of Christ and doing the works of Christ are essential aspects of being witnesses of Christ. But notice that Jesus spoke of being His witnesses. Becoming witnesses of Christ, by being filled with His Holy Spirit, is preliminary to everything we may say or do as His witnesses.

Christlike

The practical goal of Christian living is to be Christlike, and nothing so enables us to be Christlike as being filled with His Spirit. When we are filled with the Holy Spirit, we live under the Spirit's control. This does not mean the Holy Spirit will seize control of your life against your will. But when you are filled with the Spirit, you voluntarily submit to His control.

Spiritually Equipped

When you are filled with the Holy Spirit, yielded to the Spirit's control, you are spiritually equipped to be a witness of Christ. The blessing of being filled with the Holy Spirit enables you to go beyond your ordinary self in likeness to Christ, in service to Him, and in truly Christlike ministry and testimony to others. The fruit of the Spirit will be more and more evident in your life.

Capacity for Christian Living

Christians who are filled with the Spirit, and thus controlled by the Spirit, are not yet perfect (Philippians 3:12). But they do have a capacity for Christian living they would not have otherwise. Under the control of the Holy Spirit, people have amazing love; exceptional wisdom; boundless forgiveness; extraordinary courage, mercy, and compassion; and incredible endurance.

Applying the Truth

MY DAILY WALK WITH GOD

Think about this: What do you expect of a person who is filled with the Holy Spirit? Give your response to each of the following questions:

What kind of character do you expect a person to have who is filled with the Holy Spirit?____________________________

____

____

What kind of speech do you expect to hear from a person who is filled with the Holy Spirit?____________________________

What kind of deeds do you expect to see done by a person who is filled with the Holy Spirit?

Think about this: What you expect of others who are filled with the Holy Spirit, you should also expect of yourself.

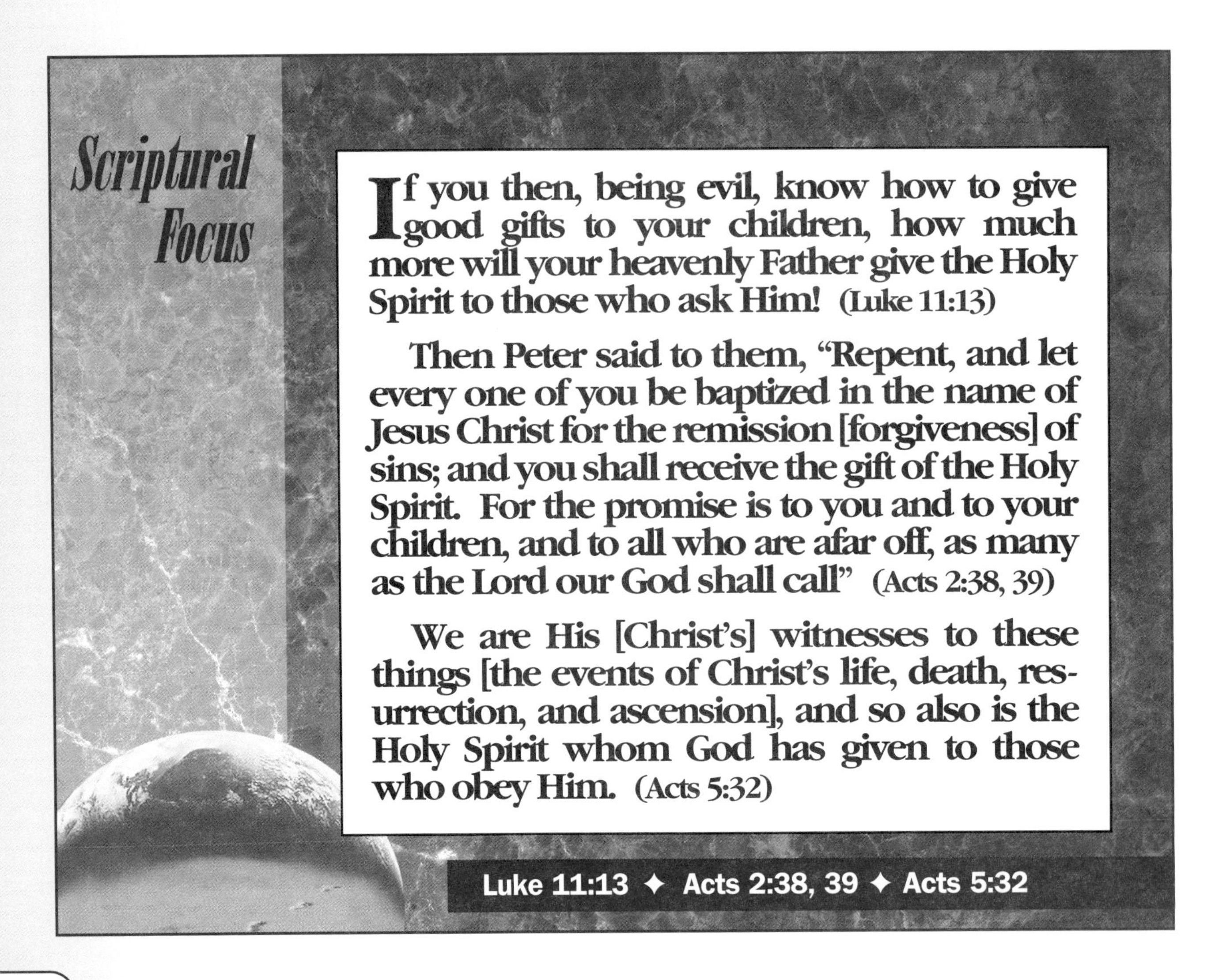

HOW TO BE A SPIRIT-FILLED CHRISTIAN

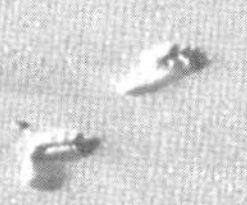

Fullness of the Spirit

The fullness of the Spirit is for every person who is saved from sin by repentance and faith in Jesus Christ. No one can be filled with the Holy Spirit who is not first born of the Spirit and sanctified (consecrated to God) by the Spirit.

If you are seeking the baptism in the Holy Spirit, persist until you are filled with the Spirit (Luke 11:9-13; 24:49). In your seeking to be filled with the Spirit, be "continually . . . praising and blessing God" (Luke 24:53) and engaged "in prayer and supplication" (Acts 1:14) for the gift of the Holy Spirit.

Seeking to be Filled

Keep in mind that God gives the Holy Spirit "to those who obey Him" (Acts 5:32). When the apostle Peter spoke to the multitude of inquiring Jews on the Day of Pentecost (Acts 2:5, 14, 38), he said they would have to believe in Christ and obey the gospel to receive the gift of the Holy Spirit. When the apostle Paul encountered disciples of John the Baptist at Ephesus, he required them to be baptized in water, thus confirming their faith in Christ and obedience to the gospel, before he would pray for them to receive the gift of the Holy Spirit (Acts 19:1-7).

Surrender

Complete surrender to Christ is the heart of how to receive the baptism in the Holy Spirit. After receiving the baptism in the Spirit, continuing daily submission to Christ is the only way to live a Spirit-filled life.

Applying the Truth

MY DAILY WALK WITH GOD

What is my answer? Self-examination:

- Do I really want to be filled with the Holy Spirit? Am I ready to turn loose of everything in my life that is unlike Christ?
- Do I want to be filled with the Holy Spirit more than I want my own way—my pride, selfishness, bitterness, wrath, sinful pleasures, and evil thoughts?
- To be filled with the Holy Spirit, what will I allow Christ to do with my life?Am I willing to say yes to Christ, whatever He asks of me, wherever He leads?

LESSON REVIEW

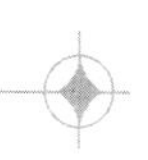

In what way, if any, has your understanding of what it means to be filled with the Holy Spirit been enhanced or changed by this lesson? ____

____

Which truth presented in this lesson do you think will be most helpful to you for Spirit-filled living? ____

____

____

What will be your practical response to this lesson?

a. Your immediate response: ____

____

____

b. Your continuing response: ____

____

____

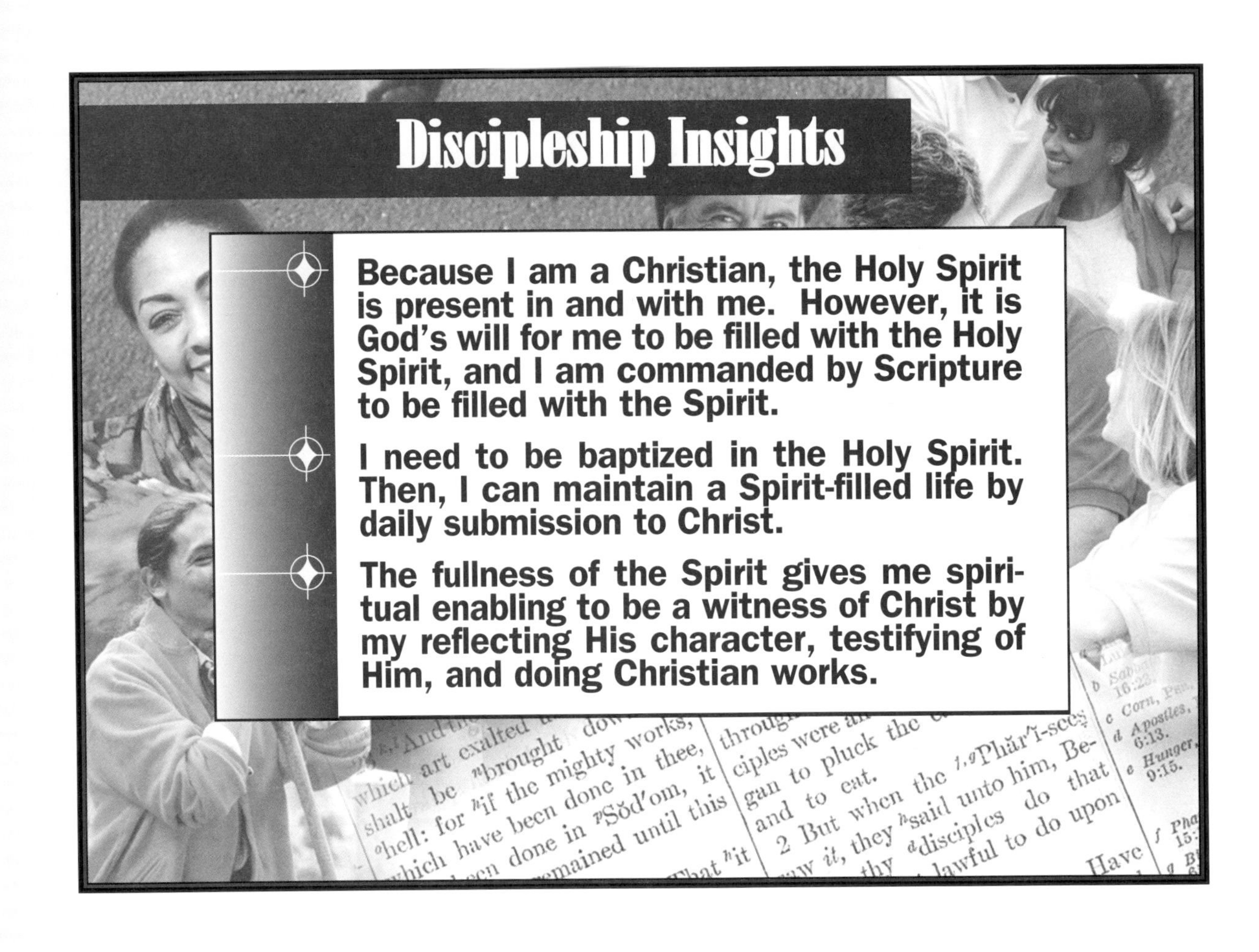

Disciplesship Insights

Because I am a Christian, the Holy Spirit is present in and with me. However, it is God's will for me to be filled with the Holy Spirit, and I am commanded by Scripture to be filled with the Spirit.

I need to be baptized in the Holy Spirit. Then, I can maintain a Spirit-filled life by daily submission to Christ.

The fullness of the Spirit gives me spiritual enabling to be a witness of Christ by my reflecting His character, testifying of Him, and doing Christian works.

Resources

Black, Daniel L., *A Layman's Guide to the Holy Spirit*, Pathway Press, Cleveland, Tennessee, 1988.

Rhea, Homer G., Editor, *The Holy Spirit in Action*, Pathway Press, Cleveland, Tennessee, 1996.

Sims, John A., *Our Pentecostal Heritage*, Pathway Press, 1995.

NOTES:____

FAMILY

A Covenant Relationship

10
LESSON

Mary Ruth Stone

INTRODUCTION

Old Testament Emphasis

The story of God's love for the human family begins in the first chapter of Genesis. That stream of family emphasis flows throughout the Old Testament to the very last verse, which says, "And he will turn the hearts of the fathers to the children, and the hearts of the children to their fathers, lest I come and strike the earth with a curse" (Malachi 4:6).

New Testament Guidance

The New Testament assumes the established family and provides guidance regarding relationships in the home. Large portions of scripture are devoted to family histories. God made eight great covenants with humankind. Each of them was dependent to some extent on *family*. God works among the vast array of family systems across a multitude of cultures in order to execute His plan.

Scriptural Focus

So God created man in His own image; in the image of God He created him; male and female He created them. Then God blessed them, and God said to them, "Be fruitful and multiply; fill the earth and subdue it . . . "

Genesis 1:27, 28

Scriptural Focus

Be filled with the Spirit . . . submitting to one another in the fear of God. Wives, submit to your own husbands, as to the Lord. For the husband is head of the wife, as also Christ is head of the church; and He is the Savior of the body. . . . Just as the church is subject to Christ, so let the wives be to their own husbands in everything. Husbands, love your wives, just as Christ also loved the church and gave Himself for her. . . . So husbands ought to love their own wives as their own bodies; he who loves his wife loves himself. For no one ever hated his own flesh, but nourishes and cherishes it, just as the Lord does the church. . . . For this reason a man shall leave his father and mother and be joined to his wife, and the two shall become one flesh. . . . let each one of you in particular so love his own wife as himself, and let the wife see that she respects her husband. Children, obey your parents in the Lord, for this is right . . . And you, fathers, do not provoke your children to wrath, but bring them up in the training and admonition of the Lord.

Excerpts from Ephesians 5:18-6:4; for clarity, read passage in its entirety.

Stop now and pray that the Holy Spirit will bring an understanding to your mind regarding God's plan for the family.

GOD: THE DESIGNER OF FAMILY

Creation Story

Chapters 1 and 2 of Genesis give the Creation story and sets forth God's design. Humankind was created male and female. God judged that Adam's aloneness was "not good" and created a woman. When Eve was brought to Adam, his response was overwhelmingly positive: (fill in the blanks) "This is now bone of _______ and flesh of ___ ______ . . . Therefore a man shall _________ his father and mother, and be ____________ to his wife, and they shall become _______" (2:23, 24).

Adam and Eve
First Couple

Adam and Eve accepted their "one-flesh" commitment to each other and their joint commission to "multiply" and "subdue" and "rule over." Neither male nor female could multiply and fill the earth alone; neither could he or she have dominion over it alone. The first couple had an idyllic relationship without superiority or subservience. They were complete only in each other. Except for sin, their relationship would have continued in that egalitarian and orderly fashion.

Reflect on that initial meeting between Adam and Eve. Can you visualize it? List some of the feelings you think they might have had:

amazement __________ __________ __________ __________

_________ __________ __________ __________ __________

_________ __________ __________ __________ __________

Pattern for Marriage

Thousands of years and many generations later, Jesus came. He reaffirmed the pattern for marriage that was established in the Garden of Eden. "And He answered and said to them, 'Have you not read that He who made them at the beginning made them male and female,' and said, 'For this reason a man shall leave his father and mother and be joined to his wife, and the two shall become one flesh'? So then, they are no longer two but one flesh. Therefore what God has ________________ ________________, let not man __________'" (Matthew 19:4-6). The triune God established the family, and Jesus reaffirmed it.

GOD: THE MODEL FOR FAMILY

God Is the Source

All that is positive on earth is patterned after heaven. Family is no exception. The family is an earthly entity with heavenly origin. God is the source and the model.

Paul wrote: "For this reason I bow my knees to the Father of our Lord Jesus Christ, from whom the whole family in heaven and earth is named" (Ephesians 3:14, 15). This being true, it follows that we must study the attributes of God and His Son in order to see what He intends the earthly family to be.

Foundation for Family
Love

The essence of God is ______________ (1 John 4); the foundation for family is the same. This godlike, unconditional, *agape* love is described in 1 Corinthians 13.

Applying the Truth

MY DAILY WALK WITH GOD

Take time to read 1 Corinthians 13 now. Pray and ask God to impart genuine, *agape* love to you. Ask Him how you might express this to your family. List ideas.

"I will show my love to my family this week by ____________

____

____

____."

Triune Godhead
A Perfect Family

The triune Godhead is a perfect family. The classical preacher, G. Campbell Morgan, made the following observations in his sermon *The Home*: "The Bible reveals Him in His fatherhood, the Bible reveals Him in His motherhood. In fatherhood as truth, strength forever caring; in motherhood as grace, essential comfort forever strengthening. Further, the Bible reveals Him as trinity in unity, the duality completed in the Son, who in the fullness of time appeared in human history, and men beheld Him, and this selfsame apostle wrote of Him, 'We beheld his glory, the glory as of the only begotten of the Father, full of grace and truth.' Thus He was the revealer of fatherhood and motherhood.

"All these things are eternal in God, without beginning and without end: fatherhood, motherhood, and sonship. We never begin to understand fatherhood or motherhood or childhood on earth until we see that these things are all the image and the likeness of that which is essential and eternal in God."

Read Romans 8:12-17 and reflect on your role as a son or daughter of God. How does this spiritual adoption make your feel?

I feel ____

____

____.

Love

It is imperative that the Christian family strives to be Godlike in its relationships. And since "God is love," love must be the essence of family. Within the Godhead the Father eternally loves the Son, the Son eternally receives and returns that love, and the Holy Spirit is the eternal medium of that love.

Trust

Deep trust is another necessary element of the godly family. The Father trusted the Son with the entire plan of salvation. Jesus executed the plan perfectly. Jesus trusted the Father enough to pray in Gethsemane: "O My Father, if it is possible, let this cup pass from Me; nevertheless, not as _ ____, but as ___ ____" (Matthew 26:39). When salvation was complete, Jesus trusted the work of the Spirit enough to say to His disciples: "It is to your advantage that I __ ____; for if I do not go away, the Helper will ___ ____ to you; but if I depart, I will ____ Him __ ___" (John 16:7). This is a model for mutual trust between spouses and between parents and children.

Do you trust your spouse completely? Are you teaching your children to be trustworthy by trusting them and by gradually increasing their responsibilities and their choices?

Hope

The home also fosters hope and makes plans for the realization of that hope. The potential for the development of each individual family member should be recognized, planned for and accomplished. And that hope should encompass eternity, not just the earthly life span.

Applying the Truth

MY DAILY WALK WITH GOD

Reflect on the future. Describe how you hope your family will be in five years.____________________________________

____

____

____

What are you doing to facilitate this hope?________________

____

____

____

Rest

In addition to love, hope, trustworthiness and much more, God is the source of rest, comfort, refuge and solace. And the family that is named after Him should provide the same. Regardless of negative experiences outside the walls of the home, the family should always provide loving refuge.

Unity

The unity of God is clear. Jesus said: "I and My Father are one . . . the Father is in Me, and I in Him . . . And he who sees Me sees Him who sent Me . . . He who has seen Me has seen the Father" (John 10:30, 38; 12:45; 14:9).

The New Testament uses the unity of the Godhead as an analogy to the marriage relationship. In 1 Corinthians, Paul compares the marriage relationship to that of Christ and the Father: "The head of every man is __________, the head of woman is ___________, and the head of Christ is ________ (11:3). Christian families are included in the prayer of Jesus for all believers: "...that they all may be ________, as You, Father, are in Me, and I in You; that they also may be _________ in Us, that the world may believe that You sent Me. And the glory which You gave me I have given them, that they may be ________ just as We are __________: I in them, and You in Me; that they may be made perfect in ___________, and that the world may know that You have sent Me, and have ___________ them as You have ___________ Me" (John 17:20-23).

It is clear that the Godhead exists in unity. It is clear that the first family was created in God's image. It is clear that Jesus intended the church to be united. It follows then that families should live in that same unity that Jesus prayed for and that Paul taught.

Mutual Submission

The Godhead provides the ultimate model for the Christian family, and the New Testament describes the orderly family. The basis for family order is the mutual submission required of all Christians in Ephesians 5. In that chapter, marriage is compared to the relationship between Christ and the church.

There has been much discussion about the meaning of *submit* in Ephesians 5:22. The word in verse 22 is the same word used in verse 21 where submission is required of all believers, both male and female. Dissension sometimes arises when people interpret Ephesians 5:22 in light of Genesis 3:16. To put those scriptures together out of context can be confusing. Genesis 3:16-19 is a curse. It is a prophecy about the consequences of original sin. It is not a commandment or a commission. Husbands should not enforce the curse by controlling and ruling over their wives. Neither should wives enforce the curse by making men "sweat" or by planting "thorns and thistles" in their husband's gardens.

Biblical Headship

Another source of disagreement is the meaning of the word *head* in Ephesians 5:23. It is not something harsh and authoritarian, because Christ is not harsh and authoritarian. Accepting the headship of a husband becomes easy for a wife when . . .

- ☐ He loves her as Christ loved the church.
- ☐ He is willing to give his life for her, not just to save her life but to develop her to her fullest potential as she is compared to a church without blemish.
- ☐ He loves her as he does his own body.
- ☐ He loves her as he loves himself.
- ☐ He nourishes her and cherishes her as Christ does the church.
- ☐ He leaves mother and father for her.
- ☐ He joins himself to her alone as one flesh.

That is Biblical headship.

Wives, have you accepted your husband's "headship"? ☐ Yes ☐ No

Husbands, check the attributes of headship listed above. How many of them do you fulfill? Mark the ones at which you excel with a check. Mark the ones you need to work on with an asterisk (*).

The Principle of Obedient Children

Order in the family requires obedient children. The fifth of the Ten Commandments demands such, and Ephesians 6:2 reaffirms it. God authored the principle of obedient children. But it is up to parents to inspire obedience. Children do not come preprogrammed to obey.

Parental Love

God inspires obedience from His children by extending unconditional love. Jesus said to the adulterous woman: "Neither do I _______ you; go and sin no more" (John 8:11). Parents inspire obedience in the same manner. Agape love is not dependent upon good behavior. Effective parental love is consistent with 1 Corinthians 13.

If parents are to be obeyed, rules and expectations must be:

☐ Reasonable

☐ Appropriate for the developmental level of the child

☐ For the good of the child and not for prideful gratification of parents

☐ Based on Scripture

☐ Explained so the child understands

☐ Based on a perception of each individual child's temperament, interests and abilities

☐ Flexible.

Parents, check the positive attributes above that your family rules follow. Which ones do you want to work on more? Place an asterisk (*) by them. Pray that God will give you a heart like His toward your children.

Children are commanded to obey parents, but wise, loving parents are responsible to inspire them to do so.

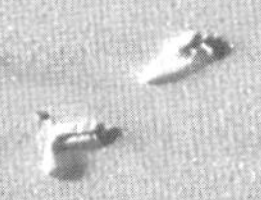

GOD: THE FAMILY COVENANT MAKER/KEEPER

Through the course of Scripture, God made eight great covenants with humankind, and each of these covenants was dependent upon the family.

Edenic Covenant

First came the Edenic covenant of Genesis 1:28-30 in which man and woman were to be fruitful and multiply and subdue and rule over. In return, God would feed them. The covenant was with man and wife, and the command to multiply indicated children.

Adamic Covenant

Second was the Adamic covenant after the Fall. This covenant in Genesis 3:15 promised: "And I will put enmity between you and the woman, and between your seed and her Seed; He shall bruise your ________, and you shall bruise His __________." Once again the descendants, the future family members, were involved as God promised that the progeny of Adam and Eve would bruise the head of the serpent.

Noah and His Sons

The third covenant in Genesis 9:8-17 was to Noah and to his sons. "And as for Me, behold I establish My covenant with you and with your __________ after you" (v. 9). And He reminds us of that covenant each time we, the descendants of Noah, see God's rainbow in the clouds.

Abrahamic Covenant

The fourth covenant was the great Abrahamic covenant in which God promised Abraham, "I will make you a great nation . . . To your descendants I will give this land . . . One who will come from your own body shall be your heir" (Genesis 12:2,7; 15:4). And on and on God spoke promises to Abraham for his seed. He stated and restated His covenant.

Finally, in Genesis 22:16-18, God told Abraham, "By Myself I have sworn...because you have done this thing, and have not withheld your son, your only son, in blessing I will bless you, and in multiplying I will multiply your __________ as the stars of the heaven and as the sand which is on the seashore; and your __________ shall possess the gate of their enemies. In your seed all the nations of the earth shall be blessed, because you have obeyed My voice."

Mosaic Covenant

The Mosaic covenant rescued not just Moses but everyone who dwelt inside the houses with the blood of the Passover lamb on the doorposts. In it God demanded the sacrifice of the firstborn. In the Ten Commandments He dealt with marital fidelity and parental respect. The Israelites were admonished to teach the provisions of this covenant to their children.

Palestinian Covenant

In the Palestinian covenant of Deuteronomy 30 and 31, the choice of life or death was for the entire family.

Davidic Covenant

In the Davidic covenant of 2 Samuel 7:16, God promised David, "And your house and your kingdom shall be established forever before you. Your throne shall be established forever." And we know that David's eventual heir was the Messiah, Jesus Christ. This covenant too was dependent on the family.

New Covenant

Now we have a new covenant found in Hebrews 8:7-13. Once again this covenant is with the "house" of Israel and the "house" of Judah. "For this is the covenant that I will make with the ________ of Israel after those days, says the Lord: I will put My laws in their mind and write them on their hearts; and I will be their God, and they shall be My people" (v. 10). Now the covenant is written on each individual heart. But all the promises of God are written to the family as a group and to each member of it as an individual.

God still has a covenant with the family! The very fact that He has kept every covenant He has ever made guarantees that He will keep His covenant with you and your family as well. There is no recipe whereby children and spouses can be predestinated, but there is a covenant—keeping God to whom they can be committed!

Applying the Truth

MY DAILY WALK WITH GOD

Do you know that God loves your children more than you do?

List some evidence of the love of God for your children.

____

____

____

____

____

____

Covenant Responsibilities

According to this same model, family members have a covenant responsibility to one another. It is binding and includes all aspects of life. The family begins with "leaving and cleaving." These words suggest both physical-sexual union and spiritual-emotional union. Marriage should be satisfying and ever growing. While marriage serves sexual, social and economic purposes, it is much more. Husbands and wives are:

✦ Husbands and Wives

☐ Helpers (Genesis 2:18)

☐ Companions (Malachi 2:14)

☐ Providers (Proverbs 31:10-31; 1 Timothy 5:1-8)

☐ Givers of themselves for the development of each other (Ephesians 5:25-33).

Spouses, check the roles above that you fulfill with your spouse. Mark with an asterisk (*) the roles you need to perfect.

This covenant is modeled by God and is sanctioned by Him (Matthew 19:6).

✦ Parents

Parents have a covenant responsibility to children:

☐ To teach them (Deuteronomy 6:l7; Proverbs 22:6)

☐ To provide for them (2 Corinthians 12:14)

☐ To nurture them (Ephesians 6:4)

☐ To discipline them (1 Timothy 3:4)

☐ To love them (Titus 2:4).

Parents, which of the above responsibilities do you carry out effectively with your children? Check them. Mark an asterisk (*) by the ones you need to work on in the future. Commit to doing it.

Parents must never break covenant with their children. In the parable of the Prodigal Son, the father remained faithful to both the sinful son and the son that was always with him (Luke 15:11-32).

Read this story again. Picture you and your family in this situation. List the emotions you felt as you read and as you visualized yourself in one of these roles.

Emotions:____________ ____________ ____________ ____________

____________ ____________ ____________ ____________

♦ **Children**

Children, in turn, have a covenant:

☐ To honor parents (Exodus 20:12)

☐ To respect them (Proverbs 23:22)

☐ To obey them (Ephesians 6:1-3).

Children, even if you are adults, do you fulfill these responsibilities? Which ones do you need to improve?

♦ **Extended Family**

The extended family has mutual responsibilities as well. Children and nephews are mentioned as having primary responsibilities for widows (1 Timothy 5:4). And where the extended family leaves off, the church family takes over.

The covenant of family is one of mutual love, support, and commitment. Changes in societal views of marriage and family do not free believers to break any part of the family covenant.

GOD: THE FAMILY PROBLEM SOLVER

Family Sins

Families have experienced problems ever since the Fall in the Garden of Eden. The first sin of disobedience was followed by murder when brother killed brother. That was succeeded by a myriad of family sins—polygamy, lusts, drunkenness, nudity, cursings, pride, lying, jealousy, greed, sodomy, gang rape, incest and desertion—all in the first 21 chapters of Genesis. The family of Job, the perfect man was attacked by Satan. His children were all killed, and his wife urged him to curse God and die.

Lack of Commitment

Problems are inevitable. They often result from lack of commitment. The result is disorder in varying degrees from dissatisfaction to quarreling to separation—first emotional and later physical—to abandonment and divorce or dissolution in some form. Relationships that endure must be respected and require considerable investment by all persons involved. However, it is comforting to know that innocent victims of broken covenants can still rely on God for help. Victims of divorce and abandonment can count on God for sustenance.

Hagar was a victim. Read her story in Genesis, chapters 16 and 21.

Poor Communication

Poor communication invites problems. Communication occurs whether or not it is deliberate. It takes effort to make it positive, not negative. Communication is both verbal and nonverbal. Research suggests that less than 10 percent of spousal communication is by words alone, less than 40 percent by tone of voice, and over half of what is heard from spouses is nonverbal (body posture, facial expressions, etc.). Actions do speak louder than words!

Body Language

The next time you are with your family members, take note of your body language as well as your words. Try to transmit love through every action and expression as well as words.

Good Communication

Obviously, even family members cannot read one another's minds. So the channels of communication must be open, and people must talk in a frank and honest but loving manner.

Some simple rules for good communication in a family include:

- Avoid negative communication (Ephesians 4:29).
- Maximize positive communication complimenting and affirming one another.
- Choose the appropriate response in terms of the situation and timing. Try to perceive the other person's frame of mind and emotional need (Proverbs 15:23).
- Speak honestly, but kindly. Accept ownership of your own emotions. Communicate feelings but not in an accusatory manner (1 Peter 2:1; Ephesians 4:15).
- Practice listening from the other person's perspective. Listen without interrupting or correcting. Observe nonverbal as well as spoken messages.

Outside Pressure

Many problems develop because of pressures from outside the home. One characteristic of strong families is their ability to survive crises by "sticking together." Ecclesiastes 4:9-12 suggests that one person alone is inadequate. Two people joined together as strands of a cord may invite God to be the third strand that can withstand pressures well.

Media Messages

Pressures from outside include messages from the mass media that pervert the Word of God and desensitize one to sin. Materialistic attitudes are transmitted. Unbiblical relationships are presented as being acceptable. But the Christian is not dependent on the media for direction. Study of the Word and praying in the Spirit can sort through the media blitz giving guidance for daily decision making.

State your family philosophy regarding the viewing of TV. If you do not have a philosophy, create one in a family meeting and write it here.

____

____

____

____

____

Lovelessness

Lovelessness is a problem. If we can begin to imagine the enormity of the positive effects of love on a family, then we can begin to imagine the enormity of the negative effects of lovelessness on the family.

Love is . . .

Love is the “cleaving” of Genesis 2:24 (KJV). Love is the friendship of Song of Solomon 5:16. Love is the togetherness that makes “one flesh” of Genesis 2:24. Love is the partnership whereby one complements the other. Love is respect. Love is honoring each other as instructed in Ephesians 5:33 and 1 Peter 3:7. Love is caring. Love is faithfulness in intellectual and emotional as well as in physical relationships. Love is the living out of the Golden Rule in Luke 6:31. Love is mercy. Love speaks grace rather than condemnation as in Ephesians 4:29. Love is freedom from fear as spoken of in 1 John 4:18.

Sometimes love hurts. The purest illustration of this is John 3:16. The person who loves the most hurts the most when through death or separation love is lost.

The Answer *Jesus*

The ultimate source of family problems is sin. From the first family until today, sin has intruded. The genealogy of Jesus himself included sinners. Yet, out of those family scandals, God brought forth Jesus. The answer to family sin today is the same—Jesus. Trust Him with your most precious possession—your family!

LESSON REVIEW

The entire Bible provides both family emphasis and guidance regarding relationships in the home. From the beginning chapters of Genesis, God sets forth the establishment and design of the family. Thousands of years and many generations later, Jesus came and reaffirmed the pattern for marriage.

God is the source and model for family. It is an earthly entity with heavenly origin and its foundation is established upon unconditional *agape* love. In addition, necessary elements of the Christian family include trust, hope, rest and refuge, unity, mutual submission, Biblical headship and obedient children.

Throughout the course of Scripture, God made eight great covenants with humankind, and each of these covenants was dependent upon the family. God still has a covenant with the family and every family member has covenant responsibilities to one another. The covenant of family is one of mutual love, support and commitment.

The answer to family problems and the intrusion of sin upon the family today is Jesus Christ. We must trust Him with our most precious possession—our family.

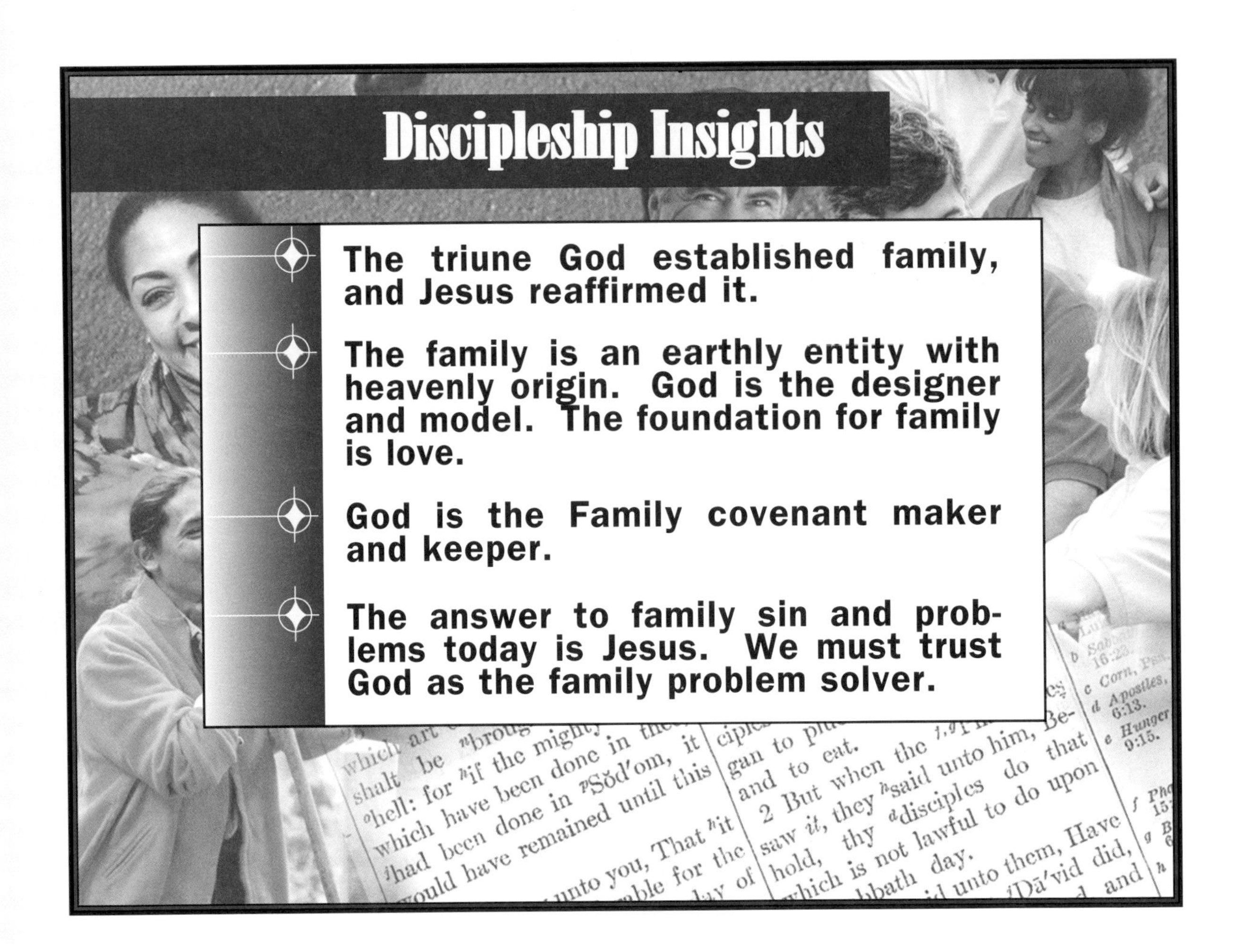

NOTES: ______________________________

The Christian Walk in the World

Ray H. Hughes, Jr.

INTRODUCTION

We are not individuals operating in a vacuum. Everything we do and say has an effect directly or indirectly on someone else. What our actions will bring to bear is determined largely by our worldview. Space will not permit an extensive study of the major worldviews such as theism, atheism, pantheism, secular humanism, new age, and others. Therefore, for our purposes here we will use the broad terms of a Christian worldview or a non-Christian worldview.

Your Worldview

It is important to note that the worldview you hold helps you interpret all of reality. It serves as a framework for sorting out and giving direction to life. If you believe in a Christian worldview you believe in an infinite personal God whose power is unlimited (Psalm 147:5). From this framework of reference, everything else in life is interpreted (Hebrews 11:6). In order to come to God we must believe that He is. This is a simple yet profound point. Belief in an infinite personal God colors all of our thoughts and directs our actions. On the other hand, a non-Christian view that no personal God exists anywhere leaves us void of any absolutes on which to base our moral standards. The universe then is self-sustaining, and man is in control of his own destiny. Thales, the Greek philosopher said, "man is the measure of himself" which goes counter to the Christian worldview which says in Jeremiah 10:23, "O lord, I know the way of man is not in himself; it is not in man who walks to direct his own steps." Thus, you can readily see how your worldview interprets all that relates to life.

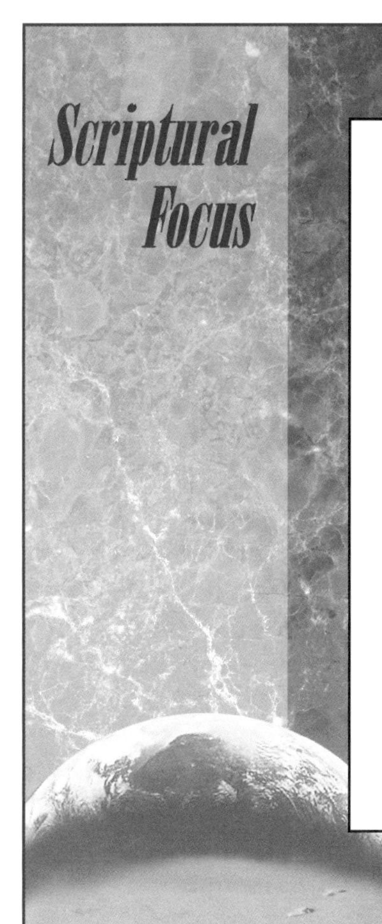

God, who made the world and everything in it, since He is Lord of heaven and earth, does not dwell in temples made with hands. Nor is He worshiped with men's hands, as though He needed anything, since He gives to all life, breath, and all things. And He has made from one blood every nation of men to dwell on all the face of the earth, and has determined their preappointed times and the boundaries of their dwellings, so that they should seek the Lord, in the hope that they might grope for Him and find him, though he is not far from each one of us; for in Him we live and move and have our being, as also some of your own poets have said, "For we are also His offspring."

Acts 17:24-28

WORLDVIEW AND VALUES

A Christian Worldview

Our present society does not seem to be aware that the worldview you hold determines your opinions and direction on the major issues of life. A Christian worldview determines that God has set certain standards that are absolute regardless of the circumstances. For example, God made us in His own image (Genesis 1:26). Therefore, we respect human life. Those values, which respect the sanctity of life, must be protected and upheld regardless of human philosophy. If you believe this premise you will search the Scriptures on these issues and come to a conclusion which will support a Christian worldview.

Below we will discuss values in the context of four global issues.

ABORTION

Abortion

The abortion issue is not just a political issue (Roe vs. Wade). It is a Christian issue as well. Only God can create life. Thus, to kill an unborn child is putting to death a creation of God. There are numerous Biblical references listed below for your review, but one outstanding scripture speaks very plainly to the life of an unborn child. The Book of Jeremiah records, "Before I formed you in the womb I knew you; and before you were born I sanctified you; I ordained you a prophet to the nations" (Jeremiah 1: 5). This scripture indicates that Jeremiah was ordained for this ministry as a prophet while he was still in his mother's womb.

Applying the Truth

MY DAILY WALK WITH GOD

The following scriptures declaring conception as an act of God are provided for your review. Look up each verse. Write down the verse that speaks most clearly to you and commit it to memory. (Genesis 16:2; 17:16; 20:18; 21:2; 25:21; Ruth 4:13; 1 Samuel 1:5-6, 19-20; Isaiah 43:7; Luke 1:15; Acts 17:24-27).

____

____

____

All of the above scriptures indicate that destroying an unborn child would be ending a life created by God. Can you find other Bible verses that speak to this issue?__________________

____

____

____

Euthanasia

EUTHANASIA

The issue of euthanasia is becoming more prominent as the population ages. Already in certain countries it is common practice to end the life prematurely of an elderly or terminally ill person. Instead of a challenge to meet the needs of the elderly, they will increasingly become a problem or burden to society, especially a society that loves pleasures and cannot tolerate inconveniences. Therefore, the moral choices will be reduced to economic choices. In this environment mercy killing is endorsed under the guise that society cannot afford to care for the ailing. However, a Christian worldview dictates that God is in control of life and only God can give or take life. It is all in His hands because, " . . . in Him we live and move and have our being . . . " (Acts 17:28).

Sexual Orientation

SEXUAL ORIENTATION

The issue of sexual orientation will increasingly affect us as the gay community aggressively presses its agenda. The Christian worldview is that God made sex and it is holy within the limits of marriage (Hebrews 13:4). Sex is also a desire given of God for procreation (Genesis 1: 28). True marriages are the work of God for He joins couples together making marriage a divine institution. "Therefore what God has joined together, let no man separate" (Matthew 19: 6). According to Scripture, man is not to introduce his own plan of sexuality but to abide by God's absolute law. Unfortunately, many non-Christian worldviews allow for a perversion of this truth.

The Word of God deals clearly with the subject of homosexuality classifying it as a despicable, abhorrent sin worthy of punishment. The Biblical terminology for this sin is sodomy (1 Kings 14:24), vile affections (Romans 1:26), unnatural affections (2 Timothy 3:3), defilers of themselves with mankind (1 Timothy 1:10), and abusers of themselves with mankind (1 Corinthians 6:9). All of these scriptures describe homosexuality. In Leviticus 18: 22 homosexuality is described as an abomination. In fact, it is classified as an abomination worthy of death (20:15).

With the current passion to be politically correct our society seems destined to have homosexuality imposed on us as an alternate lifestyle. Homosexual advocates further complicate the issue by deeming any protest (no matter how sensitive) as gay bashing. In this way disagreement on the issue is not allowed by them and any further discussion or moralizing is simply handled by calling the opposing view the religious right or bigots. However, Christians must stand for Biblical principles regardless of ridicule or consequences. When dealing with this issue we must remember to love the sinner, but hate the sin. Regardless of the nature of the sin, our protesting must be done in Christian love.

PORNOGRAPHY

Pornography

Another serious threat to our society is pornography. Our homes are being bombarded daily with a steady stream of filth. What is not available through television programming is readily accessible over the Internet. Studies show that pornography becomes an addiction that leads deeper into sexual perversion. It is reported that mass murderer Ted Bundy was led into his lifestyle through pornographic literature he began viewing as a small boy. He was finally compelled to murder in order to satisfy his appetite.

We are becoming desensitized by the profusion of mass media. Bizarre sexual behavior is portrayed as the norm as daily talk shows compete for ratings. They would have us believe that in today's society there are no boundaries and virtually anything goes. Yet God has not changed; therefore, His Word has not changed. We are admonished to present our bodies as a living sacrifice, holy, acceptable to God [which is] our reasonable service (Romans 12:1). Clearly God expects us to live holy lives and keep our bodies pure and presentable as the temple of God. As Christians we believe that God lives in us. If we expect to have a relationship with Him we must love and respect one another and be full of His Spirit (1 John 4:12-13).

Transformed Life

Through the blood of Christ a believer is crucified to the world (Galatians 2:20; Colossians 3:3). You are transformed from the world by the renewing of your mind (Romans 12:2). We are no longer conformed to the world but to the image of Christ (Romans 8:29; Philippians 3:10). The word *conform* means to be formed with, or to be put into a mold. A good illustration of this relationship is seen in the transformation of a caterpillar to a butterfly. By God's grace we are changed completely into a new creature with new habits, new designs of life, new inclinations, new desires and new goals.

WORLDLINESS

Worldliness

One definition of worldliness is "misplaced affection." So any pursuit, place, or pleasure out of harmony with God is worldliness. By this definition we can determine the things the Bible classifies as worldly. We are told not to love the world nor the things which are in the world (James 4:4). Our love is to be reserved for a higher order of things (1 John 2:15, 16). A believer's affection is to be set on things above and not on things of the earth (Colossians 3:2). We are pilgrims and strangers to this present evil world (1 Peter 2:11). We are children of light; therefore, we walk in light and not in darkness (Ephesians 5:8).

Some sincere Christians, in an effort to comply with these Scriptures, impose practices upon themselves which are not Biblical. They go beyond Scripture and actually end up losing their faith. If you will stay within the bounds of the Bible and follow Scripture in all your ways, the Holy Spirit will direct your paths.

Jesus gave the pattern of our relationship to the world in His prayer in John 17. "I do not pray that You should take them out of the world, but that You should keep them from the evil one. They are not of the world, even as I am not of the world" (John 17:15, 16). When we understand that God has placed us in the world to prepare ourselves and others for a better world, it adds meaning and purpose to life. Our citizenship is in heaven and we march to the drumbeats of another world (Philippians 3:20).

AN UNDERSTANDING OF LIFE

Understanding Life

James in his Epistle asks the question, " . . . what is your life?" He then proceeds to answer his question: "It is even as a vapor that appeareth for a little time, and then vanisheth away" (James 4:14). He then gives profound advice about our lifestyle in the light of the brevity of our existence on earth. "Instead you ought to say, 'If the Lord wills, we shall live and do this or that'" (James 4:15). An understanding of the brevity of this life should influence everything we do. Our time is limited and it must be redeemed (Ephesians 5:16).

God placed us here for His glory (Isaiah 43:7), and for His pleasure (Revelation 4:11). We are His servants and belong to Him so completely that we have no individual status. We are His! He has bought us with a price. Therefore our body and spirit are His (2 Corinthians 5:19). The knowledge that He is Lord and Master leaves us no alternative but to totally commit everything to Him. Jesus expressed it in this manner to His disciples, "He who finds his life will lose it, and he who loses his life for My sake will find it" (Matthew 10:39).

MATERIALISM

Materialism

We live in a materialistic, things-oriented world. The only life that millions of people know is a life of things. They labor for things and live for things. This is the carnal, fleshly life which leads to death (Romans 8:5, 6). One factor that makes men enemies of the cross of Christ is "minding earthly things" (Philippians 3:19).

Concentrating on things causes us to be anxious, self-centered, and gives a distorted view of life. Things are fleeting and will pass away, but those who do the will of God will abide forever (1 John 2:17). Jesus gave a dissertation on life in Matthew 6. He stated that the cure for anxiety is to trust in the Father's care. In His usual teaching method, He asked the question, "Is not life more than food and the body more than clothing?" (Matthew 6:25-33). So, life does not consist in what you eat or wear, neither in the things you possess (Luke 12:15).

This is not to say that we cannot own things, but is to say that we should not let things own us. The Biblical order is, "But seek first the kingdom of God and His righteousness, and all these things shall be added to you" (Matthew 6:33).

A materialistic view of life is an enemy of spirituality. A church is not to be judged by its buildings, furnishings, or finances. Success does not rest in these things. The Laodicean church boasted that it was rich and increased in goods and had need of nothing, but they were sharply reprimanded by God who had an altogether different appraisal (Revelation 3:15-20).

WORLDVIEW AND RELATIONSHIPS

Pattern for Relationships

Life is composed of relationships—personal, family, business, church, work, play, and so forth. Jesus set the pattern for relationships. "'You shall love the Lord your God with all your heart, with all your soul and with all your mind.' This is the first and great commandment. And the second is like it: 'You shall love your neighbor as yourself'" (Matthew 22:37-39).

Our first relationship is total commitment to Him and then to others. In fact, our love toward one another is a measure of our love to God (1 John 4:20). If we claim to love God and hate our brother the Bible classifies us as liars.

RELATIONSHIPS TO EACH OTHER

Life is not a solo flight. We are dependent creatures. No man lives to himself

Relationships to Others

and no man dies to himself (Romans 14). "Two are better than one . . . For if they fall, the one will lift up his fellow . . . " (Ecclesiastes 4:9-10). This is God's divine plan for personal relationships.

Applying the Truth

MY DAILY WALK WITH GOD

The following scriptures point out our proper relationship to each other. Look them up and match them to the six statements concerning relationships.

Scriptures: James 5:16; 1 Corinthians 12:25; Hebrews 10:25; Ephesians 4:2; 1 Thessalonians 5:11; Galatians 6:2.

We are . . .

_________________ members one of another.

_________________ to bear one another's burdens.

_________________ to pray for one another.

_________________ to care for one another.

_________________ to edify one another.

_________________ to exhort one another.

The above list is by no means exhaustive, but it will provide a starting point for you to begin your studies on the subject of relationships.

FAMILY RELATIONSHIPS

Family Relationships

The Word of God is explicit about family relationships. God wants us to know our responsibilities to each other. Parents and children have mutual responsibilities to make family life successful.

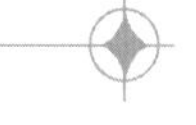

The relationship of children to parents is to obey and honor (Ephesians 6:1-3; Colossians 3:20).

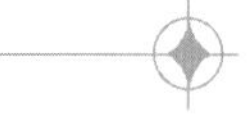

The relationship of parents to children is to . . .

a. Provoke not to wrath (Colossians 3:21).

b. Bring them up in the Lord (Ephesians 6:4).

c. Nurture (discipline) and admonish them (Ephesians 6:4).

The relationship of husbands and wives is to . . .

a. Love each other (Ephesians 5:25, 33).

b. Give ourselves to each other (1 Corinthians 7:4,5).

c. Please each other (1 Corinthians 7:33, 34).

d. Submit one to another (Ephesians 5:21; Colossians 3:18) as it is fit in the Lord.

e. Nourish and cherish (Ephesians 5:29, 33).

RELATIONSHIP TO ENEMIES

Enemies

Jesus said to love them who love us has no reward. As the children of God, we should love our enemies (Matthew 5:44-46). Therefore, where our enemies are concerned we must love them, pray for them, and bless them. If they hunger, feed them. If they thirst, give them drink (Romans 12: 20).

RELATIONSHIP TO SINNERS

Sinners

There is an unfortunate spirit of isolationism in the church. Sinners are not a part of the life of most church members. Our attitude should be one of insulation rather than isolation. The apostle Paul dealt with this in his letter to the Corinthians. We associate with the sinners but we do not participate in their sin. Life demands it (1 Corinthians 5:9). So what are we to do with this relationship?

- Be friends with them (Matthew 11:19).
- Go after them (Luke 15:7; 14:23; Matthew 9:10-13).
- Invite them to your home (Luke 5:29) and go to theirs (Luke 7:36; Luke 19:5).
- Create in them a desire for Christ.
    a. By an example (1 Corinthians 11:1).

    b. By a witness (1 Peter 3:15).
- Take them to the house of God. Nowhere is a sinner commanded to go to church; but we are commanded to bring them in (Luke 14:23).

Applying the Truth

MY DAILY WALK WITH GOD

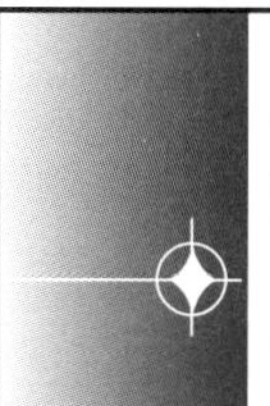

In the space below list some of the things in your life that you feel need improvement concerning your relationships. Then see if you can find a scripture in the lesson that speaks to that need.

____

Once you have completed your list, take time to pray over each point and ask God to help you with these areas of your life to bring them in line with His Word.

WORLDVIEW AND DESTINY

God's Will

What is God's plan or will for Christians? Jeremiah 29:11 says that God has a plan for our success and has our future in His hands. Many of us struggle with God's will for us, but our first concern should be to know God's will? The Word clearly states God's will:

- Sanctification is the will of God (1 Thessalonians 4:3,4).
- It is the will of God to give thanks in everything (1 Thessalonians 5:18).
- It is His will that we be filled with the Spirit (Ephesians 5:17, 18).

It is His will that we . . .

- Present bodies holy to Him.
- Have a renewed mind.
- Be separate from the world (Romans 12:1-3; Ephesians 5:10).
- Pray everywhere and lift up holy hands (1 Timothy 2:8).

Harmony with God

We must understand that God's will is always best for us, and He will give us grace to fulfill His will. When we come to know His will then we can comply with it. We must get in harmony with God. Many of us set goals and then ask God to join us in our program. We should ask, "Lord what would You have me do?" "What are You up to?" We should then tell Him, "I want to join You." That's what God wants.

- Be filled with the knowledge of His will (Colossians 1:9).
- Understand His will (Ephesians 5:17).
- Be complete in His will (Colossians 4:12).

Christ always sought to do the will of God (Psalm 40:8). He was involved in the Father's work so much that He would rather do His will than eat (1 John 4:34). His interest was pleasing the Father—"not my will but thine."

When we come to know His will, we must do it. When we do His will day by day, He directs our paths into purposeful living. It is God who works in us both to will and to do His good pleasure (Philippians 2:13).

God's Will for Your Life

No doubt at this point you are asking, "What about God's will for my life?" Find out what God is doing and join Him in that pursuit. He will work His will through you when you submit to His will from your heart (Ephesians 6:6). It will be amazing how He directs your ways. He has a plan for you and will reveal it as you do His will.

As Christians we must live our lives as if we are merely on a journey on our way to that final destination. As we go, it is our responsibility to herald the good news and let the light of Christ shine through us as He instructed before His ascension, "As long as I am in the world, I am the light of the world" (John 9: 5). In Matthew 5: 14, Christ explains that since He is now physically leaving the earth, He is leaving His light in us.

Thus we see that the values, behaviors, patterns, and relationships of an individual all interact to determine one's destiny. How we manage our lives in accordance with God's Word will ultimately decide our destiny. This means we strive to live our lives free of sin and to do the good will of our heavenly Father. We then look to live eternally with Christ in heaven as our final destiny.

LESSON REVIEW

The worldview an individual holds serves as a framework for sorting out and giving direction to life. A Christian worldwiew believes in an infinite personal God whose power is unlimited. This assertion determines that God has set certain standards that are absolute, regardless of the circumstances.

The Christian walk in the world must be based upon Scriptural principles. This daily walk must address Christian values in context of global issues such as abortion, euthanasia, sexual orientation and pornography.

It is through Christ that the believer is transformed into a new creation with new habits, new designs of life, new desires and new goals. The Christian worldview brings new patterns of relationships. These relationships include total commitment to Jesus Christ first and then to family, business, church and other encounters in life.

The values, behaviors, patterns and relationships of an individual all interact to determine one's destiny. How we manage our lives in accordance with God's Word and His plan will ultimately shape the Christian walk in the world and decide our final destiny.

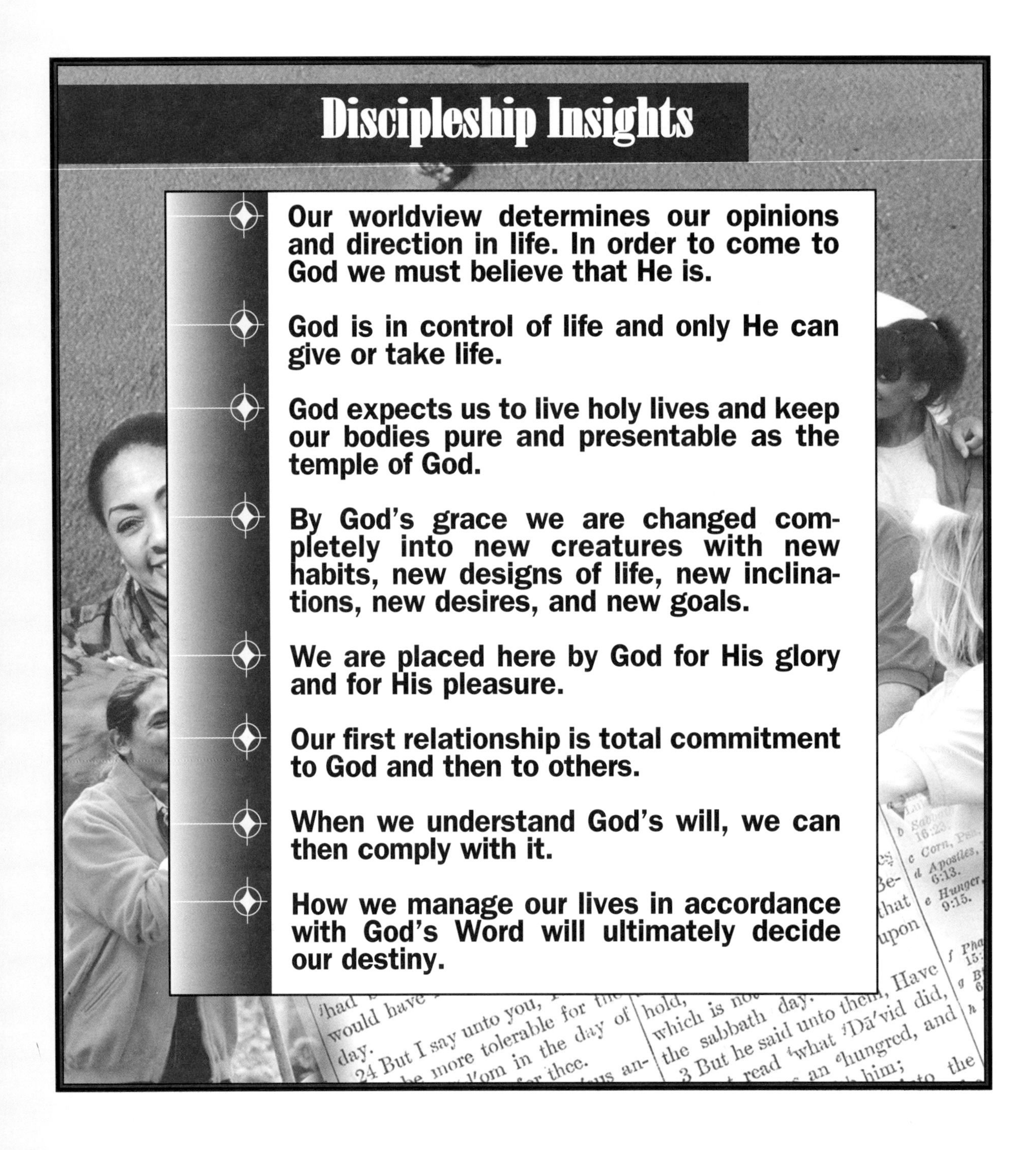

Resources

Geisler, N., and W.D. Watkins. *Worlds Apart: A Handbook on World Views*. Grand Rapids: Baker, 1989.

General Executive Council Minutes from 1984-1996 (unpublished).

Harper, S. *Devotional Life in the Wesleyan Tradition*. Nashville, Tennessee: The Upper Room, 1983.

Land, S.J. *Pentecostal Spirituality: A Passion for the Kingdom*. Sheffield, England: Sheffield Academic Press, 1994.

Middleton, J.R. and B.J. Walsh. *Truth Is Stranger Than It Used to Be: Biblical Faith in a Postmodern Age*. Downers Grive, Ilinois: InterVarsity Press, 1995.

Minutes of the 66th General Assembly of the Church of God. Cleveland, Tennessee: Church of God Publishing House, 1996.

Resolutions: Celebrating Our Heritage. A Collection of resolutions adopted by the Church of God General Assembly from 1968-1996.

NOTES:

CHURCH

Walking With Jesus in the Fellowship of the Church

12
LESSON

Mike Chapman

INTRODUCTION

"Christ . . . loved the church and gave Himself for her," (Ephesians 5:25). Every Christian must come to terms with this verse. If Jesus loved the church, so should we.

Why Jesus Came to Earth

As we read the story of the gospel found in the New Testament, we discover that Jesus came to earth to do several things. First and foremost, He came to redeem fallen humanity by His death on the cross. In other words, He came to seek and to save that which was lost (Luke 19:10). Second, He came to establish His kingdom rule on the earth through the proclamation of the good news and by destroying the works of the devil (Matthew 4:17; 10:7-9; Colossians 2:15; Hebrews 2:14; 1 John 3:8). Third, He came to establish a community—the church—that would be made up of all those who have been redeemed and who have become citizens of His kingdom (Matthew 16:18, 19). The church would be a mission outpost of the kingdom of God in the world with the authority to do the works of Jesus.

In this lesson, we will look closely at this topic. The goal is that, at its conclusion, you will love the church too.

> **Christ . . . loved the church and gave Himself for her.**

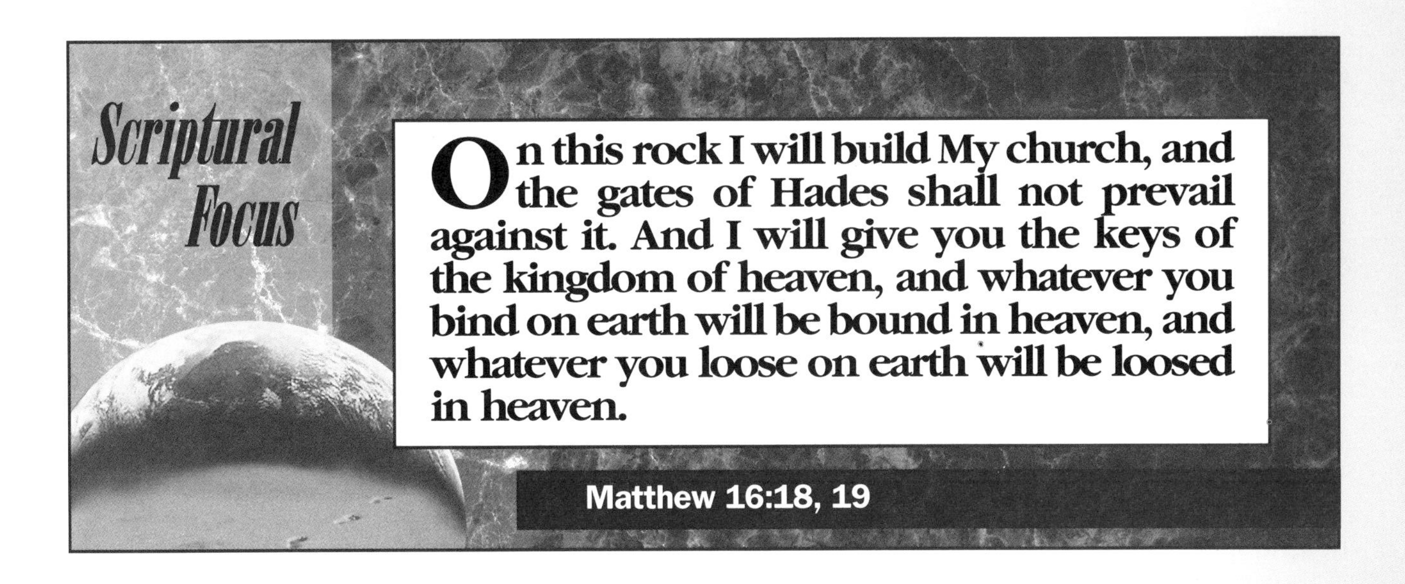

THE BEGINNING OF THE CHURCH

The Church ***A Divine Institution***

According to Jesus' own words, the church is a divine institution. It is not the product of man nor the result of societal or cultural evolution. Jesus made it clear . . . I will build my church. Jesus said His church would be built on a rock so secure that the very gates of hell would not be able to overcome it. What exactly is this rock?

Some would say that the rock is the apostle Peter. But, this does not seem correct because how could the security of the church be built on frail, imperfect humanity? Although Peter was a great man of God, he was, like all of us, prone to make mistakes and fail. No, the rock of the church has to be more substantial than this.

The rock on which the church stands is the truth that Peter confessed when Jesus asked, "Who do you say that I am?" (Matthew 16:15, 16). Jesus is the Christ, the Son of the living God! It is on this powerful truth of revelation that the church stands. It is this truth that causes hell to tremble!

The Church ***Built by Christ***

These verses also make it clear that the church is not built by men; it is built by Christ. Therefore, it is His church. While believers are laborers together with Christ (1 Corinthians 3:9), only He adds people to His church. Luke states this in Acts 2:47, " . . . and the Lord added to the church daily those who were being saved." Paul echoes this when he said, "For by one Spirit we were all baptized into one body [the church]" (1 Corinthians 12:13). This means that a person who believes on Jesus is placed into the church by the work of Christ through the Holy Spirit.

Not only does Jesus build His church, He continues to work in His church. He works to make the church holy through His Word. He sees the church as His bride whom He loves and prepares for the day of the wedding (Ephesians 5:25-27).

Keys of the Kingdom

One of the intriguing metaphors of this passage is the *keys* of the Kingdom. What exactly does this mean? First, we can assume that the word *key* refers to authority. Jesus was conferring authority on the church. The church has been given the authority to bind and loose. Now, what does that mean?

It is interesting to note that the keys are not of the church, but of the Kingdom. The kingdom of God is a major theme of the New Testament. It refers to the rule of God. Jesus often referred to His message as the gospel of the Kingdom (Matthew 4:23; 9:35; Luke 4:43; 8:1). He sent His disciples out to extend the kingdom of God (Luke 9:1-6; 10:1-11). He spent His last moments with them speaking to them about the kingdom of God (Acts 1:3), and it is obvious that this theme was a major part of the preaching of the early church, especially the apostle Paul (Acts 8:12; 19:8; 20:25; 28:23, 31).

The Church *Endowed With Authority*

The church, then, has the authority to extend the kingdom of God. We have the power to preach good news to those who are held captive in the kingdom of darkness, giving them the opportunity to become citizens of God's kingdom (Colossians 1:13; 1 Peter 2:9). We also have the authority to overcome any power of darkness that stands in the way of this purpose (Luke 9:1-6; 10:1-11; James 4:7). Because of this authority, Jesus promised that the gates of hell would not prevail against His church!

So we see that the church rests upon the foundation of faith in Jesus Christ. It is His church, endowed by Him with authority to carry out its mission. Its purpose transcends time. The church is an embassy of the kingdom of God!

Applying the Truth

MY DAILY WALK WITH GOD

What is an embassy? How does this serve as an appropriate illustration of the work of the church in relationship to God's kingdom?

____

____

____

Why is the confession that Jesus is the Son of God a significant statement and a substantial rock of the church?

____

____

____

THE CHURCH AS THE PEOPLE OF GOD

The Meaning of Church

The word *church* has come to mean different things to different people. To many, it refers to a building with stained-glass windows and a steeple. To others it is a denomination. And to still others, it is something you can watch on television. While all of these ideas express our cultural orientation, they do not touch on the true significance of the Biblical picture of the church. Biblically, the church is people of God—a called people, a covenant people and a commissioned people.

ekklesia

Over 100 times in the New Testament, the word *church* is used. Each time it is a translation of the Greek word *ekklesia*. This interesting Greek word is a compound word which means "the called out ones." The church is a community of people who owe their existence and their distinctiveness to one fundamental fact—the call of God.

God's purpose is to call out of the world a people for Himself, to redeem them from sin, and to give them a distinct identity in the world. This peculiarity is because the church is God's people (1 Peter 2:9). Peter says, "Once [you] were not a people but are now the people of God . . . " (1 Peter 2:10). Such a change in status occurs only because of the call of God.

Call to Salvation

God's call to salvation is not only an invitation to the guilty and the lonely to find forgiveness. It is also a call to find community and a new identity in Him. He calls us from isolation to be joined to a people. The church is not an aggregation—people who choose to come together. It is a congregation—people who have been called together by God to give visible and verbal expression of the kingdom of God.

A Covenant People

The church is also a community of people who are bound to one another because they are bound to God in a covenant. Therefore, it is proper to say that the church is a covenant people.

Covenants were common in the ancient world. A covenant was a contract or pact which bound friend to friend (1 Samuel 18:3) and established relationships between people. Jeremiah foretold the coming of a new covenant when God would write His law not on tables of stone, but on the hearts of a people, and these people would become His people (Jeremiah 31:33). This is the idea behind our understanding of the Lord's Supper (Communion) as a reminder of the "new covenant" (2 Corinthians 11:25; Matthew 26:28). When Communion is observed, we are reminded that through the new covenant we are one with our brothers and sisters in Christ (Ephesians 4:4-6).

As previously stated, the church exists to extend God's kingdom. This was the essence of the Great Commission in Matthew 28:18-20, "And Jesus came and spoke to them, saying, 'All authority has been given to Me in heaven and on earth. Go therefore and make disciples of all the nations, baptizing them in the name of the Father and of the Son and of the Holy Spirit, teaching them to observe all things that I have commanded you; and lo, I am with you always, even to the end of the age.'" He commissioned us to be a kingdom of priests (Exodus 19:6; 1 Peter 2:9, 10) who bring the mercy and grace of God to a fallen world.

Applying the Truth

MY DAILY WALK WITH GOD

Read carefully 1 Peter 2:9, 10:

> "But you are a chosen generation, a royal priesthood, a holy nation, His own special people, that you may proclaim the praises of Him who called you out of darkness into His marvelous light; who once were not a people but are now the people of God, who had not obtained mercy but now have mercy."

Prayerfully contemplate each phrase as it relates to your life in Christ. Briefly write in your own words what this passage of Scripture says about you.

____

____

____

____

____

____

____

____

____

THE EXPRESSIONS OF THE CHURCH

Expression of the Church

It will be helpful to consider the various expressions of the church. For our purposes we will examine three expressions: (1) the universal church, (2) the local church and (3) the denominational church.

✦ Universal

The universal church is an expression used to describe the one body of

Christ. It consists of all people throughout history who have been called to salvation through Jesus Christ and who have trusted in Him as their Savior. Simply put, you become a member of the universal church by being saved. If you are saved, you are in the church!

Some Christians think that being saved and a member of the universal church is enough. Well, in one sense it is enough. It is enough to get you to heaven. But, God wants more for His people. He has called us to assemble together in His name (Hebrews 10:25) and has assured us that when we do, He will be in our midst (Matthew 18:20). He wants us to submit to the leadership of the church for the protection of our own soul (Hebrews 13:17). He wants us to enter and enjoy relationships with other believers so we may strengthen and encourage one another (e.g., Galatians 6:2; Colossians 3:16; 1 Thessalonians 5:11; Hebrews 10:24).

✦ Local

It is this expression of the church that is mostly seen in the New Testament. Paul wrote his letters to local churches—the church at Rome, the church at Philippi, the church at Corinth, and so forth. He dealt with local church problems and local church leaders. The local church is vitally important because it is the visible expression of the universal church in its community. Therefore, a Christian who has not become a part of a local church is not completely in the will of God.

✦ Denominational

Although not found in the Bible, the denominational church is another expression of the church. Denominations are a network of churches, pastors, and believers who have joined together because of common doctrines, interests and cultures. Typically, these networks began as the result of a revival or renewal movement. As God's Spirit moved among a people, those who identified with the revival joined together, and soon a denomination would be birthed.

Denominations are not bad. In fact, there are many positive benefits of denominations. They provide for cooperative efforts in global missions, benevolent ministries and discipleship. They also provide effective structures for accountability and discipline.

Unity

Denominationalism, on the other hand, is not good. It is a divisive term which implies that one group is superior to all the others. Some have gone so far as to insinuate that members of their group are the only true Christians. Repeatedly, the Bible reminds us of the importance of striving for unity in the body of Christ (Ephesians 4:3-6). Paul urged that there be no divisions among us (1 Corinthians 1:10), and Jesus prayed that His followers would be one (John 17:11, 21).

Cooperation

A better way to relate to denominational differences is to recognize every true believer in Christ as our brother or sister and learn to appreciate the various "flavors" and "colors" within the body of Christ. Doctrinal differences among Bible-believing churches are really less significant than we think. Cooperation, rather than competition and conflict, is much more Christ-honoring.

Applying the Truth

MY DAILY WALK WITH GOD

If you have a close friend who is part of another denomination or church, arrange to meet with them for a friendly discussion of their church's doctrine on such topics as "What is the Bible?" "How is a person saved?" "Who is Jesus Christ?" "What is heaven like?" You may be pleasantly surprised by how much you agree.

BECOMING A MEMBER OF THE CHURCH

Church Membership

We now come to a very important matter. Are you a member of a local church? Remember, if you are a believer, you are already a Christian and are a member of the universal church, the body of Christ. However, God desires for you to unite with a local church. What will this entail?

Joining a local church is an act of testimony and commitment. First, it is a testimony. When you join a local church, you are testifying that you are born again and that Jesus is your Savior. Joining a local church does not make you a Christian, but it is a vital and important step. It makes your faith in Christ official and public.

Water Baptism

Water baptism is closely associated with church membership. In baptism, you are following Christ's command (Matthew 28:19). You are continuing the pattern of the earliest Christians (Acts 2:41). You are giving a visible reenactment of the gospel (Romans 6:3-10). While faith in Christ is what brings salvation, water baptism should not be considered optional for a Christian. You should be baptized as a testimony of your faith.

Commitment

Joining a local church is also a commitment. It is a commitment to the people of God with whom you share the new covenant. It is a commitment to spiritual authority (1 Thessalonians 5:12, 13; Hebrews 13:17). It is a commitment to involvement in ministry. When Jesus added you to His church, He gifted you to serve. When you join a local church, you bring your giftedness to that body so you can participate in the church's mission (Romans 12:6-8; 1 Peter 4:10, 11). Joining a local church is also a commitment to support the church financially through tithes and offerings (Malachi 3:10; 1 Corinthians 16:2; 2 Corinthians 9:6-10).

Enrichment

Joining a local church is an enriching experience. A local church will provide you with meaningful worship experiences where you can join in corporate praise to God and hear His Word preached and taught. You will be provided spiritual care and support during your times of need. Opportunities for fellowship and the building of relationships with fellow believers will also be afforded to you. The local church will become for you a catalyst of spiritual growth and development.

Applying the Truth

MY DAILY WALK WITH GOD

Have you been baptized in water since you accepted Christ as your Savior? If you have not, speak to your pastor about the next opportunity for water baptism. (Note: When you are baptized, why not invite several of your unsaved friends to come to your baptism. What a great opportunity to share your faith with them!)

If you have not joined a local church, ask God to lead you to the local church He wants you to be a part of. Make an appointment to speak to the pastor about joining. You'll be glad you did!

LESSON REVIEW

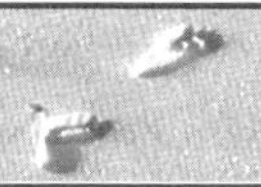

Discipleship

Jesus loved the church and gave Himself for it. Do you love His church? Are you willing to be baptized and unite yourself with a local church so you may join His kingdom enterprise on the earth? Discipleship is not walking alone. It is walking in fellowship with other believers in a body called the church!

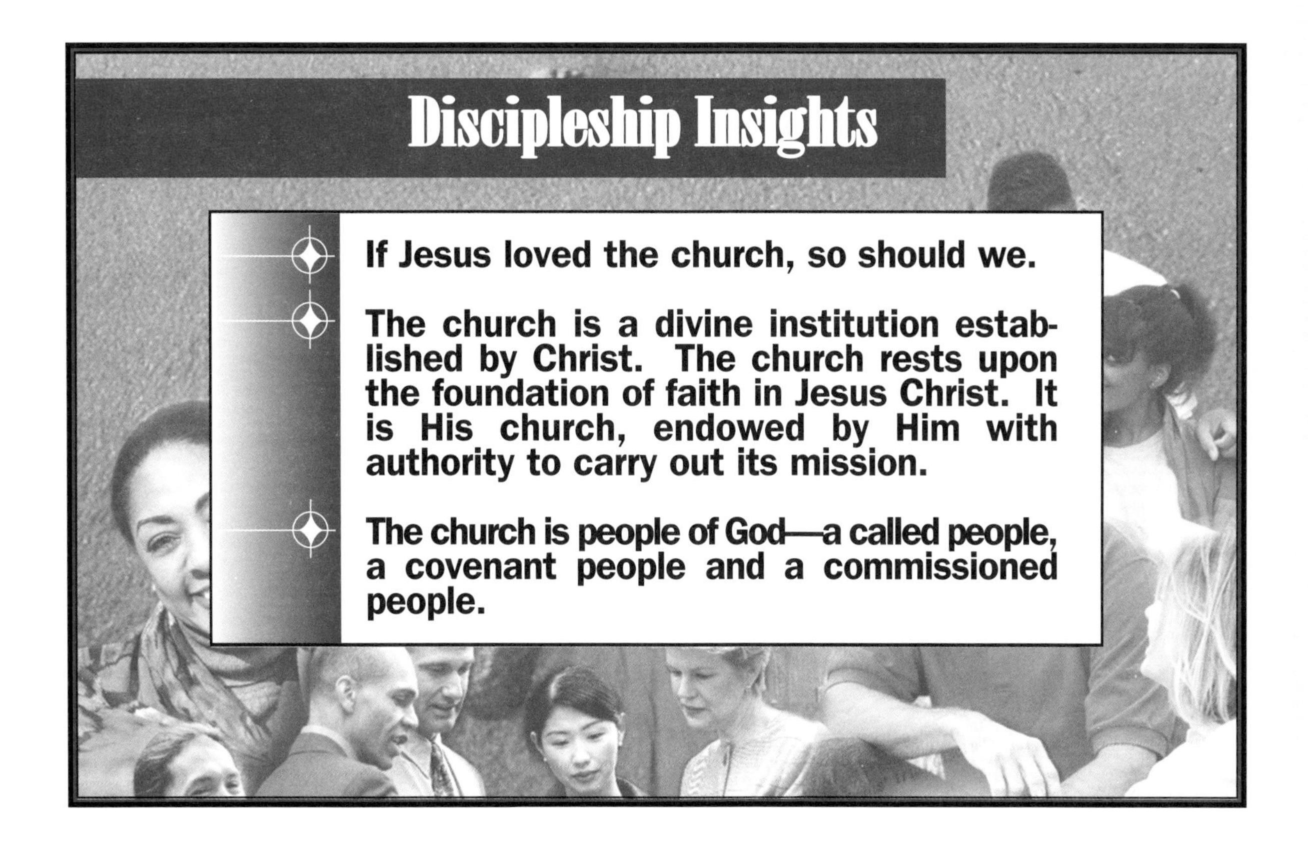

Discipleship Insights

If Jesus loved the church, so should we.

The church is a divine institution established by Christ. The church rests upon the foundation of faith in Jesus Christ. It is His church, endowed by Him with authority to carry out its mission.

The church is people of God—a called people, a covenant people and a commissioned people.

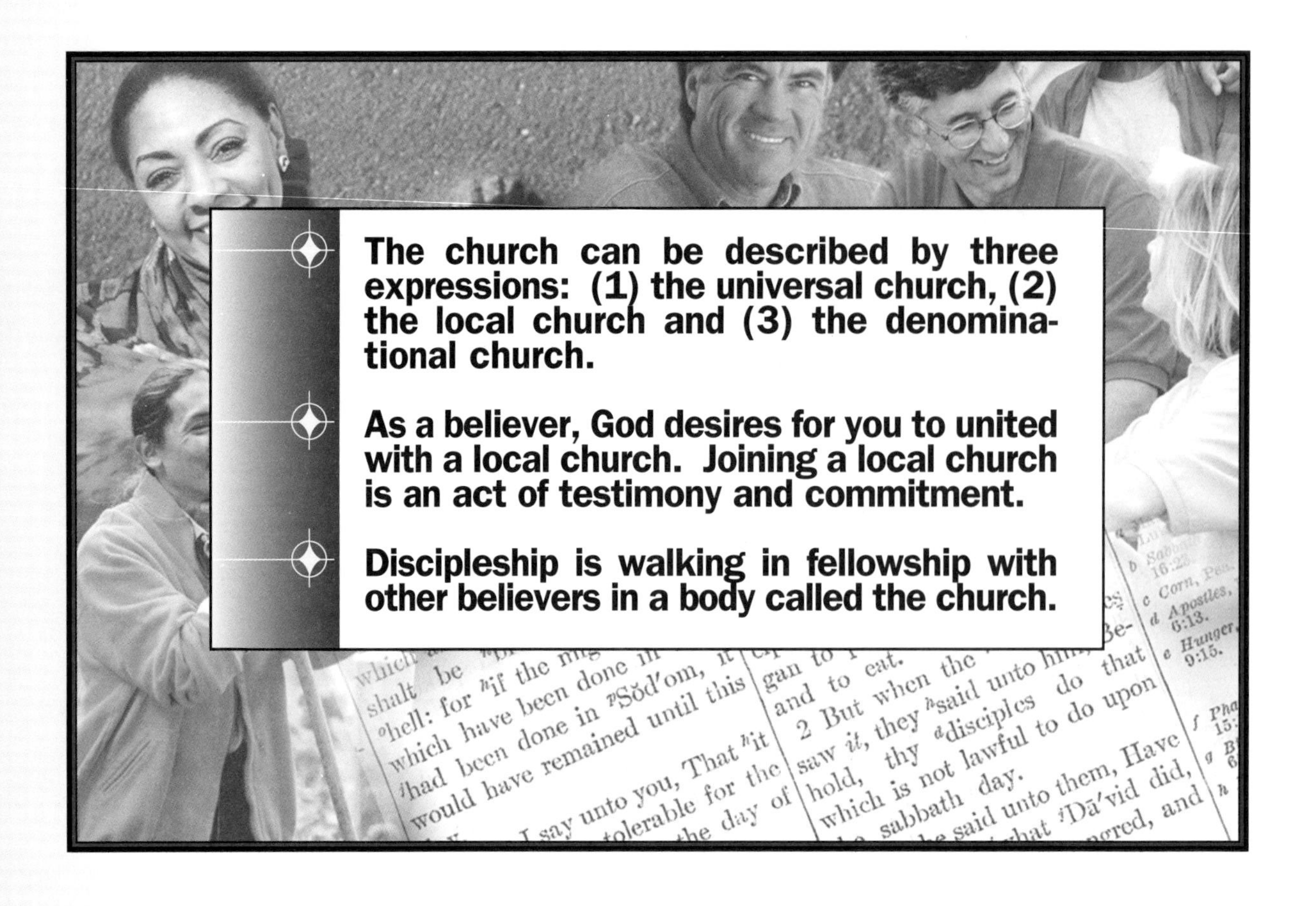

Resources

Arrington, French, *Christian Doctrine: A Pentecostal Perspective* (Volume 3), Cleveland, Tennessee: Pathway Press, 1994.

Chapman, Mike, *Discipleship: Developing the Christlife, Life in the Church*, Cleveland, Tennessee: Pathway Press, 1989.

Chapman, Mike, *Discover Your Spiritual Gifts*, Cleveland, Tennessee: Church of God Department of Lay Ministries, 1993

Conn, Charles W., *Like A Mighty Army*, Cleveland, Tennessee: Pathway Press, 1996.

Getz, Gene, *Sharpening the Focus of the Church*, Chicago: Moody Press, 1973.

Giles, Kevin, *What on Earth Is the Church?,* Downers Grove, New Jersey: InterVarsity Press, 1995.

Snyder, Howard, *The Community of the King*, Downers Grove, New Jersey: InterVarsity Press, 1977.

NOTES:____